# Grazing & Feasting boards

THEO A. MICHAELS

# Grazing & Feasting boards

50 fabulous sharing platters
for every mood and occasion

PHOTOGRAPHY BY
MOWIE KAY

RYLAND PETERS & SMALL
LONDON • NEW YORK

*Dedicated to my darling wife Anna and kids Eva, Lex and Luca. And the dog – Belle, she hates being left out...*

CREATIVE DIRECTOR Leslie Harrington
EDITORIAL DIRECTOR Julia Charles
EDITORS Gillian Haslam & Kate Eddison
HEAD OF PRODUCTION Patricia
    Harrington
FOOD STYLIST Kathy Kordalis
PROP STYLIST Lauren Miller
INDEXER Hilary Bird

Published in 2022
by Ryland Peters & Small
20–21 Jockey's Fields
London WC1R 4BW
and
341 E 116th St
New York NY 10029
www.rylandpeters.com

ISBN: 978-1-78879-466-4
10 9 8 7 6 5 4 3 2 1

Printed and bound in China.

CIP data from the Library of Congress has been applied for. A CIP record for this book is available from the British Library.

## NOTES

• Both British (metric) and American (imperial plus US cups) measurements are included in these recipes; however, it is important to work with one set of measurements and not alternate between the two within a recipe.

• Uncooked or partially cooked eggs should not be served to the very old, frail, young children, pregnant women or those with compromised immune systems.

• When a recipe calls for the grated zest of citrus fruit, buy unwaxed fruit and wash well before using. If you can only find treated fruit, scrub well in warm soapy water before using.

• Always sterilize jars to be used for storing homemade preserves and sauces before use. See page 29 for instruction on ways you can do this.

• Food safety: ensure your serving board or platter is clean, food-safe and heat-proof if necessary before use. Rub wooden surfaces with olive oil to avoid staining and choose non-porous surfaces for oily or juicy foods.

# CONTENTS

# INTRODUCTION

In my role as an Executive Chef I've been creating grazing experiences for many years now. These have ranged from intimate boards for two people to share by candlelight, to huge feasting tables for 250 plus corporate diners. This book is the culmination of all my experience to date, laid out and presented to you in one place.

In the following pages you'll find my blueprints for 50 themed grazing boards and sharing platters to suit every occasion, from a family night spent in front of the TV to effortless entertaining over drinks with friends, and ranging from the humble to the spectacular. Some offer outrageous fun, others sophisticated elegance. Each sharer is designed around a theme and I've listed everything you need to recreate these beautiful edible works of art at home. I invite you to use the list of suggested ingredients as a guide (making any substitutions you like to suit your own tastes or audience), follow my simple recipes, or buy in ready-made versions for maximum convenience. Then using the beautiful photographs as your main inspiration, with encouraging guidance and tips from me on the sidelines, build your boards with confidence and creativity. I couldn't resist including some of my favourite recipes, but I offer you these as suggestions only – not rules – so feel free to swap out ingredients, or combine elements from different boards to create something you love.

Sharing food is one of life's great pleasures, it's something that I touch upon in almost every cookbook I've created and something we try to do as a family as often as possible – it's good for the soul. The concept of 'breaking bread' is thousands of years old and I, for one, believe it to be at the very heart of being human. It's eating together that cultivates our relationships with friends and family and gives us the platform to spend time together. My boards are the very definition of bringing people together and enable you to create shared memories over delicious food, spectacularly presented in a fun, interactive way.

# HOW TO BUILD YOUR SHARERS

## CONSIDER YOUR BOARD CAREFULLY

Over the years I've used a variety of surfaces as boards. You can't beat a wooden chopping or bread board for a small sharer, or a piece of plywood for something larger. (If you rub olive oil into the wood this helps protect the surface from staining.) Trays are also useful, especially the 'butler' style with a shallow lip and handles, which are most convenient for times when you may be casually snacking on the sofa, rather than a flat board, which works best when stationary on a table, as items may wobble and fall off. When you are including oily or juicy food, a non-porous surface like slate or ceramic works best. But as long as what you choose is clean, food-safe and heat-proof, if necessary, you're good to go!

## USE COLOUR EFFECTIVELY

Consider colours carefully, from the surface of the board to the food itself. Use shades that work within your theme, from the board to the small dishes and serving tools. Or, if your board is all one type of food, such as cheese, and seems a bit flat, take a step back and see where you could add bursts of colour to liven it up, either with small dishes of accompaniments or fresh garnishes, such as herbs.

## CREATE VISUAL 'ANCHORS'

Boards work best when they have a few visual 'anchors', by which I mean larger pieces of food (or in some cases it might be bowls of dips or sauces), that add structure and give definition. Always position these first and build the board up around them, remembering to consider whether your board will be seen from the front only or from all sides.

## POPULATE THE SPACE

Once the big stuff is in place, you can start to fill the spaces in between. Also, remember to keep wet ingredients away from dry. Arrange overlapping lines of bread, crackers or cookies; these can also act as useful barriers between, say, cheese and cold meats, or savoury and sweet. Next add clusters of any medium-sized foods. Odd numbers work best for visual displays so arrange things in clusters of three, five and so on.

## HOT STUFF

Ensure food that is to be eaten hot is added last and build up your board in advance leaving a gap for it. I often put a swirl/smear of condiment on the surface as a placeholder for the hot item, then it's good to go as soon as the hot stuff is added.

## MIND THE GAPS

When the board starts to fill up, it is time to move on to the smallest items; placing a handful of olives, grapes or nuts into some of the gaps, or small bundles of radishes or salad leaves and so on.

## CONSIDER THE CONDIMENTS

I often wipe and smear these straight onto my boards, but you can also place them in small ramekins and pots with spoons. Position them conveniently close to the foods they pair with, so cheese next to chutney, ham next to mustard.

## ADD FINAL FLOURISHES

Use sprigs of fresh herbs, citrus slices and wedges and edible flowers and dot about to add colour and freshness. Adding a drizzle can be a nice touch too, to add flavour as well as visual interest: balsamic glaze, flavoured oils, sweet syrups and sauces can all work. Keep all the garnishes edible to avoid possible confusion and/or food poisoning!

# CHAPTER
## 1

# Lazy Brunches

# OVERNIGHT OATS TRAY

Overnight oats are a great way to get a headstart on a healthy breakfast and make for a colourful and fun sharer. I've given three ideas for flavour variations here to get you started, but really you can experiment and flavour or top the oats with any fruits, nuts and spices you like.

### RED BERRY OATS

50 g/½ cup rolled/ old-fashioned oats

125 ml/½ cup whole/ full-fat milk

1 tbsp chia seeds

2 tbsp natural/plain Greek yogurt

2 tbsp runny honey

**For the toppings**

65 g/½ cup fresh berries, such as raspberries, blueberries and/or hulled strawberries

3 tbsp natural/plain Greek yogurt

1 tbsp sunflower seeds

1 tbsp runny honey

a few sprigs of fresh mint

### MATCHA COCONUT OATS

50 g/½ cup rolled/ old-fashioned oats

125 ml/½ cup coconut milk

1 tbsp chia seeds

2 tbsp agave syrup

1 tsp matcha powder

**For the toppings:**

2 tbsp toasted coconut shavings

a pinch of matcha green tea powder

### TURMERIC CHAI OATS

50 g/½ cup rolled/ old-fashioned oats

125 ml/½ cup full-fat/ whole milk

1 tbsp chia seeds

2 tbsp natural/plain Greek yogurt

2 tbsp runny honey

¼ tsp ground turmeric

**For the toppings:**

1 tbsp pistachio kernels

a pinch of dried rose petals (optional)

### PRESENTATION

*a wooden breakfast tray with cut-out handles and a rim works well here*

### EACH VARIATION MAKES 1 JAR/SMALL BOWL so scale up to create as many servings as you need

Mix all the ingredients together (except the toppings) in a small cereal bowl or Kilner/ Mason jar or similar. Cover the bowl with a small plate (or seal the jar with its lid) and put in the fridge for at least 3 hours, or ideally overnight. When you are ready to serve, give the oats a stir to mix and add a splash of liquid to loosen, if the mixture seems too thick. Scatter over the toppings and arrange on a tray to serve.

### HOW TO ASSEMBLE

For a breakfast in bed special occasion, add some colour and wow factor to the tray with a bed of freshly prepared fruit, as pictured (you can follow the ingredients list on page 17 or choose whatever you fancy).

# RAINBOW FRUIT PLATTER

Fresh, vibrant and delicious – all the things I want in a fruit platter. I've made this one with my favourite fruits to create a beautiful rainbow of goodness. Simply add a bowl of creamy Greek yogurt and a piece of fresh honeycomb to create an indulgent treat. (Pictured on pages 14–15.)

1 cantaloupe melon, quartered and sliced into thin wedges

1 blood orange or red grapefruit, cut into 8 wedges

2 passion fruit, halved

2 kiwi, halved

4 physalis/cape gooseberries

400 g/14 oz. black grapes, snipped into 2–3 small bunches

100 g/⅔ cup fresh cherries with stems

100 g⅔ cup each berries, such as blueberries, blackberries, raspberries and strawberries

400 g/1¾ cups natural/plain Greek yogurt

60 ml/4 tbsp runny honey

200-g/7-oz. piece of natural honeycomb

100 g/1 cup pecan halves (optional)

a few sprigs of fresh mint

**PRESENTATION**
*a large oval platter works well here, either ceramic or metal. If you use metal, line with a sheet of baking parchment cut to size to prevent the acids present in some fruits reacting with the metal*

**SERVES 4-6**

Wash and prepare all of the fruit. Don't rush at this – use sharp knives and cut it cleanly. Handle berries with care so as not to squash them. Discard any stones and pips and gently pat the fruit dry with some paper towels.

**HOW TO ASSEMBLE**

Decide where you are placing the yogurt and put a small shallow bowl in position.

Start arranging the largest pieces of fruit first, such as the melon slices and blood orange wedges. Add the passion fruit and kiwi halves, with the cut sides facing upwards. Dot the bunches of grapes around the platter and add the physalis/cape gooseberries.

Next fill in all the gaps with the smaller fruits, such as the berries and cherries, so the board looks full and abundant. Cover and chill (or keep somewhere cool) until ready to serve.

When ready to serve, add the pecan halves (if using) and garnish with a few sprigs of fresh mint. (Do not be tempted to do this too early, the nuts will lose their crunch and the mint will become floppy.)

Lastly, spoon the Greek yogurt into the bowl on the platter, drizzle the honey over the top and put the honeycomb piece in the middle.

# BUILD-YOUR-OWN
# PANCAKE STACK

My memories of being a kid in New Jersey are mainly of eating American-style pancakes topped with melted butter, lashings of whipped cream and maple syrup. At home now we all love pancakes and this is how we make them – big and fluffy with all the trimmings, and with a choice of savoury and sweet toppings, or both at the same time! The secret to a tasty pancake board is to keep everything warm until you're ready to assemble it. This is my tried-and-tested easy pancake batter recipe, easy enough for my kids to make too so I urge you to give it a go.

300 ml/1¼ cups double/heavy cream

1 tbsp icing/confectioner's sugar

12 rashers/slices streaky bacon

50 g/3½ tbsp butter, melted

6 eggs (any size)

100 g/1 cup each of blueberries and raspberries

200 g/2 cups strawberries, hulled and halved if large

2 bananas, peeled and sliced on the diagonal

salt and freshly ground black pepper

edible flowers, to garnish (optional)

### PANCAKES

700 ml/3 cups whole/full-fat milk

1 tbsp cider vinegar

300 g/2¼ cups plain/all-purpose flour

1 tbsp baking powder

1 tbsp sugar

a pinch of salt

1 medium egg

25 g/¼ stick butter, melted

**SERVES 4-6**

For the pancake batter, pour the milk into a jug/pitcher, add the vinegar and set aside while you mix together the dry ingredients – it will curdle slightly but that's fine.

Combine the flour, baking powder, sugar and salt together in a mixing bowl, then crack the egg into the bowl – don't mix yet. Now pour in the milk and vinegar mixture and whisk until just smooth. Pour in the melted butter and mix until incorporated. Once done, leave the pancake battere to rest for 15 minutes, this gives the baking powder a chance to aerate the batter; add more flour or milk to get a nice thick consistency (you want it to be slightly thicker than double/heavy cream).

Meanwhile, whisk the double/heavy cream with the icing/confectioner's sugar until it holds its shape, then cover and chill.

Preheat the oven to 80°C fan/100°C/210°F/Gas ¼.

Fry or grill/broil the bacon until crispy and transfer to a plate. Cover with kitchen foil to stop it drying out and keep warm in the low oven.

Grease a heavy based frying pan/skillet with a little of the butter and place on a medium-high heat. Using a ladle add a portion of batter (about 125 ml/½ cup) and without moving the pan leave it to cook for a couple of minutes until the pancake firms up and you see holes appearing on the top. Using a spatula, flip the pancake over and cook for a minute. Place the pancake on a plate, cover with kitchen foil and keep warm in the low oven. Continue until all the batter is used up.

*a wooden board is ideal here, such as a large chopping board or bread board. You can cover it with a sheet of baking paper for an easier clean up, if liked*

Find a small oven-safe pan or a heat-proof bowl for the scrambled eggs and pop it in the oven to warm. Add a little more butter to the pancake pan and put on a high heat. Whisk the eggs, season generously with salt and pepper and pour into the pan. Gently move the eggs around the pan as they cook, they'll be done in a couple of minutes. Once cooked, transfer to the warm serving pan or bowl, cover with foil and set aside (do not put them in the oven, they may overcook and turn rubbery).

## HOW TO ASSEMBLE

Melt the remaining butter in a small pan or in the microwave. Start with the warm pancakes, overlapping them in a line down the centre of the board (as pictured) or arranging them in stacks, as preferred, and drizzle with the melted butter.

Arrange the banana slices and the berries on either side of the pancakes. Remove the bacon and eggs from the oven, and keeping the sweet and savoury elements separate from each other as far as possible, add them to the board.

Spoon the whipped cream directly onto the board or into a small bowl, place on the board and drizzle with a little maple syrup. Put the remaining syrup in a small jug/pitcher and add to the board for people to help themselves. Garnish with a few edible flowers, if liked.

Encourage everyone to take a few pancakes and top with whatever they fancy, finishing with a drizzle of syrup and dollops of whipped cream.

# BUILD-YOUR-OWN
# BAGEL BOARD

Enjoy your brunch bagel your way with my build-your-own board; simply offer up a selection of bagels alongside a choice of fillings to enjoy. This board is super-easy to assemble using mostly pre-made ingredients, but I do whip up a cream cheese with chives and horseradish which takes seconds and elevates it all nicely. Buy fresh bagels from a bakery if you can, it does make a difference.

230-g/8-oz. tub/package of cream cheese

1 tbsp snipped chives

1 tbsp creamed horseradish

a squeeze of lemon juice

6 fresh bagels (any type)

150 g/5¼ oz. smoked salmon

200 g/7 oz. pastrami or salt beef, sliced

100 g/3½ oz. salami or chorizo

100 g/3½ oz. Cheddar, sliced

a knob/pat of butter

a few tbsp Dijon mustard

1 avocado, peeled, stoned/ pitted and sliced

1 precooked candy or regular beetroot/beet, sliced

1 buffalo (steak) tomato, sliced

½ cucumber, sliced

2 Cos/Romaine lettuces, leaves separated

about 20 large caperberries

2–3 fresh figs, halved

a few sprigs of dill or flat-leaf parsley, to garnish

**SERVES 4–6**

**PRESENTATION**
*a wooden board is ideal here, such as a large chopping board or bread board*

To make the whipped cheese, put the cream cheese in a bowl and beat until fluffy. Transfer half to a small serving dish, cover and chill. Add the snipped chives and horseradish with a squeeze of lemon juice to the remaining whipped cheese in the bowl and beat to combine. Transfer to a separate small serving dish, cover and chill.

**HOW TO ASSEMBLE**
Start by arranging the bagels in lines down the centre of the board, overlapping. (You can leave them whole or split them, as preferred.) Arrange the smoked salmon, cold meat slices and Cheddar slices on the board in groups, separating out the slices and overlapping them. Position the condiments and accompaniments close to what they complement (i.e. mustard next to the cold meats, caperberries with the salmon), either directly on the board or in small dishes. Add the dishes of cream cheese, placing the one with the horseradish closest to the salmon. Finally, add the butter and fresh salad ingredients to fill the spaces, with an eye on the colours being spread around the board and keeping any wet ingredients away from the bagels so as not to make them soggy. Sprinkle over some herbs to garnish, and serve.

# ALL-DAY BRUNCH SHEETPAN

There's a reason this is called an all-day brunch – you can have it anytime of the day! I've included things I love, but feel free to add or remove elements to suit your own tastes. For instance, you can omit the sausages and bacon and add slices of pan-fried halloumi for a veggie version. If you don't have a waffle-maker simply substitute store-bought toasting waffles. Do however always serve with freshly squeezed OJ and hot coffee.

8–12 chipolata sausages

6–8 Portobello mushrooms

2 on-the-vine cherry tomato stems (about 16 tomatoes)

a little olive oil

8 rashers/slices smoked streaky bacon

12 fresh asparagus spears

400-g/14-oz. can baked beans

a pinch of smoked paprika

a splash of vegetable oil

4–6 eggs (any size), depending on appetite

1 avocado, peeled, stoned/ pitted and sliced

maple syrup, to drizzle

### WAFFLES

300 ml/1¼ cups whole/full-fat milk

1 tsp malt vinegar

200 g/1½ cups plain all-purpose flour

1 tbsp baking powder

1 tbsp caster/superfine sugar

a pinch of salt

1 medium egg

25 g/¼ stick butter, melted

### PRESENTATION
*a large rimmed sheetpan is ideal, but a clean one!*

### SERVES 4–6

Preheat the oven to 190°C fan/210°C/410°F/Gas 6.

For the waffle batter, pour the milk into a jug/pitcher and add the vinegar; it will curdle slightly, but that's fine. Combine the flour, baking powder, sugar and salt in a large mixing bowl (no need to sift the flour). Pour the milk and vinegar mixture into the flour, add the egg and whisk together. Once combined, whisk in the melted butter, a few lumps is okay. You want a thick consistency, so add more flour or milk as needed. Leave to rest for 15 minutes to let the baking powder aerate the batter.

Arrange the sausages, mushrooms and tomatoes on a baking sheet. Drizzle with a little olive oil and season. Cook in the preheated oven for a total of 20 minutes. After the first 10 minutes of the cooking time, add the bacon then after 15 minutes, add the asparagus. Remove the sheet from the oven and cover in foil to keep everything warm.

Meanwhile, warm the baked beans in a saucepan, transfer to a serving bowl or pan (as pictured) and dust with smoked paprika. Fry the eggs in a frying pan/skillet with a little oil on a high heat so they crisp around the edges. Remove from the pan and drain on paper towels.

Preheat your waffle maker following the manufacturer's instructions. Lightly oil the plates using a brush and when ready to use, ladle in just enough batter to cover the plates; close the lid, turn it over and leave to cook to the set time (usually about 6–8 minutes). Keep the waffles on a plate, cover with kitchen foil and keep warm. Continue until all the batter is used up.

### HOW TO ASSEMBLE
Arrange all the cooked items in distinct groups on the clean sheetpan. Add the avocado slices and a small bowl of maple syrup. Place the hot waffles on the sheet last and serve immediately with freshly brewed coffee and orange juice or even a few bubbles if it's gone noon...

# CONTINENTAL BREAKFAST BOARD

A continental-style breakfast should be light but satisfying, with protein-rich cheese and cold meats to graze on, as well as mouth-watering pastries and sticky preserves. You can warm up ready-made pastries for 3–5 minutes in a low oven, or look out for chilled or frozen ready-to-bake ones and follow the instructions on the package to prepare – worth it for that lovely freshly baked smell! (Pictured on pages 26–27.)

3 eggs (any size)

honeydew melon, nectarines, plums, persimmom, apricots, or other fresh fruit of your choice

8–12 French pastries, such as croissants, pains aux chocolat, pains aux raisins

a few slices of white or granary sourdough bread

150 g/½ cup natural/plain Greek yogurt

2 tbsp runny honey

2 tbsp walnut pieces, toasted

edible flowers, to garnish (optional)

4 tbsp each of blackcurrant preserve, marmalade (or Rustic Citrus Preserve, see recipe opposite) and chocolate hazelnut spread

8–12 slices French Torchon ham, German Brunswick ham and/or Prosciutto

6–8 slices Emmental, Gruyère and/or Jarlsberg

175-g/6-oz. Brie de Meaux, or similar

a knob/pat of butter, chilled

**PRESENTATION**
*a generously sized wooden charcuterie board with a handle works well here*

**SERVES 4–6**

Add the eggs to a saucepan of boiling water and cook for 7 minutes, then remove and rinse under cold running water. Once cool, peel and rinse each egg, then halve lengthways, season with a pinch of sea salt and set aside until needed.

Meanwhile, wash and prepare the fruit, slicing the stone fruits and persimmon in half and slicing the melon thinly.

Either warm or cook the pastries in the oven, as required (see above). Toast the sourdough bread and cut each slice in half.

**HOW TO ASSEMBLE**

Spoon the Greek yogurt directly onto the board, using the back of the spoon to make swirls, or spoon into a ramekin or small pot, if preferred. Drizzle over the honey and sprinkle with walnuts and edible flowers (little thyme flowers are nice here), if using. Decant the preserves and chocolate hazelnut spread into ramekins or small bowls and dot these around the board. Add small spoons and a honey dipper for serving.

Arrange the hams and cheeses on the board, separating and fanning out the slices and placing the whole Brie near an edge where it can be easily cut. Add the eggs halves in groups of three.

Arrange the warm pastries and toasted sourdough in groups around the board. Place the butter directly onto the board.

Add the fruit last, arranging the melon in slightly overlapping slices and dotting the other fruits around to fill in any gaps. Keep the melon away from the pastries as it will make them soggy. Serve at once while the pastries are still warm.

# RUSTIC CITRUS PRESERVE

This is my go-to recipe when we have glut of oranges to use up – it couldn't be easier to prepare and uses every part of the fruit except the pips. It just takes 10 minutes to bring it all together, then leave to cook slowly for about 1 hour and 20 minutes. A little bit of effort makes a big impression.

600 g/1 lb. 5 oz. unwaxed
   oranges (about 4)

1 unwaxed lime

500 g/2¼ cups caster/
   granulated sugar

350 ml/1½ cups water

**MAKES 2 X 385-ML/
5½ FL OZ. JARS**

Wash the oranges, quarter them lengthways, (remove the pips) and finely slice widthways. Do the same for the lime. Give the oranges and lime a little squeeze as you put them into a heavy based saucepan to help release their juices, then add all of the remaining ingredients.

Bring to a rolling boil, then reduce to a bubbling simmer for about 1 hour and 20 minutes, stirring occasionally to stop it catching. The preserve will thicken a lot once cooled. Decant into sterilized jars (see below).

This preserve will keep for 3 months once sealed but keep refrigerated once open and use within 7 days.

**HOW TO STERILIZE JARS**
Dishwasher – put the jars and lids through a hot cycle and once dry fill them with your preserve.

Microwave – hand wash the jars, don't dry them and microwave for about 1 minute or until fully dry and submerge the metal lids in boiling water for a few minutes.

Oven – hand wash the jars, don't dry them and place into pre-heated oven for 10 minutes at 160°C fan/140°C/275°F/Gas 1 and submerge the metal lids in boiling water for a few minutes.

# 'JARCUTERIE' BUFFET

These grab-and-go 'jarcuteries' are a fabulous choice for a brunch party, as everyone can pick the jar they fancy and no plates are needed. I've chosen three of my favourite salads and down-sized them, but you can experiment with any flavour combinations you like. You can buy in most of these ingredients and just assemble. Start saving those jars!

## CHICKEN CAESAR SALAD

1 chicken breast

1 tbsp dried oregano

1 ciabatta roll

olive oil, for brushing

1 Little Gem/baby Romaine lettuce

150 g/5¼ oz. Parmesan, shaved into thin slivers

6 anchovy fillets, drained and each sliced into 3 strips

150 ml/⅔ cup Caesar salad dressing

6 hard-boiled quail's eggs, peeled and halved

## HOUSE SALAD

½ small cucumber, cut lengthways into 3 large batons

6 mini breadsticks

a few sprigs of rocket/ arugula

9 red grapes

a handful of unsalted mixed nuts

9 green olives, pitted

3 gherkins/dill pickles

25 g/1 oz. salami, thinly sliced

100 g/3½ oz. hard cheese, such Manchego or Cheddar, cut into 3-cm/ 1-in. cubes

1 pear, peeled, halved and thinly sliced

100 g/3½ oz. firm blue cheese, such as

Roquefort or Danish Blue, cut into thin wedges

50 g/1¾ oz. Parma ham, thinly sliced

1 on-the-vine cherry tomato stem, snipped into 3 small pieces

## SESAME TUNA AND AVOCADO

1 tsp wasabi paste

250 g/9 oz. fresh tuna steaks

2 tbsp mixed white and black sesame seeds

3 spring onions/scallions

1 pinch chilli/chili powder

2 avocados

200 g/7 oz. cooked sushi or basmati rice

175 g/6 oz. edamame beans

1 medium courgette/ zucchini

For the dressing:

3-cm/1-in. piece of fresh ginger, peeled and grated

2 tbsp light soy sauce

a pinch of sugar

1 tsp rice vinegar

**MAKES 9 (3 OF EACH RECIPE)**

### PRESENTATION
*you will need 9 clean and dry glass jam/jelly jars and 12 wooden/bamboo skewers, and a tray or board that will take them*

## CHICKEN CAESAR SALAD

Butterfly the chicken breast in half and cut into 6 strips. Season with salt and pepper and a pinch of dried oregano and thread onto 3 of the wooden skewers (presoaked). Place onto a hot griddle pan for 2 minutes on each side or until cooked through, then set aside.

Cut the ciabatta roll into long slices that are taller than the jar (you may need to halve them lengthways if too wide) and brush with olive oil. Place onto a hot griddle pan to char for 30 seconds on each side, then remove from the pan and set aside.

Cut the lettuce lengthways into 3 wedges and fan out the leaves a little but without detaching them from the stalk end. Wedge a few slithers of Parmesan and 12 of the anchovy strips inbetween the leaves. Drizzle a little dressing over the top followed by some cracked black pepper.

Drizzle just enough dressing into each jar to cover the base.

Place a slice of charred ciabatta into each jar, followed by a wedge of dressed gem lettuce, then a chargrilled chicken skewer. Shave some more long strips of Parmesan and carefully place into the jars with a few sticking out, wedge in the quail's eggs halves, add the remaining anchovy slices and finally drizzle some more dressing over the top.

### HOUSE SALAD

Place one baton of cucumber, two breadsticks and a few sprigs of rocket/arugula into each jar. Drop in three grapes, a few nuts and three olives to sit in the lower half of the jar. Skewer a gherkin/dill pickle, then a chunk of hard cheese, finishing with a folded piece of salami and place into the jar. Add a few slices of pear, then some wedges of blue cheese and folded pieces of Parma ham. Finish with a few cherry tomatoes on the vine sat on top of the jar.

### SESAME TUNA AND AVOCADO

For the sesame tuna, loosen the wasabi paste with 1 teaspoon of water then brush it over the tuna steaks. Sprinkle the sesame seeds and chilli/chili powder onto a plate and press the tuna steaks into the sesame seeds to fully coat. Place onto a hot griddle pan to sear for 1 minute on each side, then remove and let rest for a few minutes. Carefully cut the tuna steaks into clean, neat cubes and thread about 3 onto each skewer.

Trim the spring onions/scallions and place onto the hot griddle pan and char for 30 seconds on each side then remove. Depending on their thickness, halve these lengthways.

Carefully cut the avocados in half, peel, stone/pit and slice lengthways.

For the dressing, mix together the grated ginger, soy sauce, sugar and vinegar with a pinch of salt and reserve.

Mix 1 tablespoon of the sesame seeds into the precooked rice. Pat down a layer of the rice at the bottom of each jar, followed by a layer of edamame beans. Place a charred spring onion/scallion into each jar, sticking out slightly.

Using a vegetable peeler, make a few long courgette/zucchini shavings and twirl a couple into each jar along with a few slices of avocado. Finally position one or two sesame tuna skewers into each jar and finish with a drizzle of the dressing.

### HOW TO ASSEMBLE

When your jars are ready, simply line up all nine jars equally spaced on the board or tray and serve! If you have any leftover salad ingredients, such as tomatoes or lettuce, arrange those amongst the jars to decorate and add colour.

# CHAPTER
# 2
# Everyday Sharers

# SALAD BAR BOARD

I've always been a sucker for a salad bar! Using a good variety of salad leaves adds colour, contrasting texture and flavour. This works well as a side with pizza, but if you like you can also add a protein element, such as hard-boiled eggs, diced cheese, canned tuna, cubes of precooked chicken breast or slices of smoked salmon, to make the board more substantial.

2 iceberg or Cos/Romaine lettuces

1 Gem/Boston lettuce

1 raddichio lettuce, leaves separated

1 carrot

250 ml/1 cup each of French vinaigrette or honey and mustard dressing, Thousand Island dressing and blue cheese dressing

½ cucumber, cut into thick slices

200-g/7-oz. can sweetcorn/corn kernels, drained

1 (bell) pepper, thinly sliced

2 large handfuls of baby plum tomatoes

1 red onion, thinly sliced

100 g/3½ oz. precooked (pickled or steamed) candy or regular beetroot/beets, sliced

For the toppings:

200-g/7-oz. jar sliced jalapeño peppers, drained

200 g/7 oz. crispy fried onions

300 g/10½ oz. mixed black and green olives

400-g/14-oz. can mixed bean salad, drained and rinsed

**PRESENTATION**
*a large wooden board,
3 ramekins or small dishes*

**SERVES 6–8**

Trim the edge of the iceberg, Cos/Romaine, Gem/Boston lettuce and radicchio stalks for a clean cut, then remove any loose outer leaves. Slice the lettuces into 2.5-cm/1-in. thick slices, cutting through the stalk so they hold together. (Alternatively, separate the lettuce leaves.)

Using a vegetable peeler, shave the carrot into long ribbons.

**HOW TO ASSEMBLE**

Arrange the prepared lettuce on each end of the board.

Pour the three salad dressings into individual ramekins or small bowls and place on the board. Add small serving spoons, if you wish.

Dot the different salad ingredients in bands or clusters directly onto the board to fill the space in the middle. I prefer to group them by colour to create a rainbow effect. As there are a lot of different ingredients here, keep each one in its own band or cluster i.e. arrange all the sliced (bell) peppers in one group and all the sweetcorn/corn kernels together in another.

Once the main salad ingredients are all laid out on the board, load some of the lettuce with a selection of the toppings. Again group colour with colour – green olives with the green lettuce, black olives with the radicchio and so on – then serve up a rainbow for everyone to enjoy!

# BUILD-YOUR-OWN
# CHEESE PLATE

A good cheese plate should offer a variety of textures and flavours of cheeses and be accompanied with tasty savoury nibbles to cut through the richness of the cheese, plus a good variety of chutneys or jellies to add interest. And don't forget the crackers. You can theme a board by country i.e. all French or all Italian cheeses, all British, all American, and so on, or take your queue from the seasons as to your accompaniments (fresh fruit in summer, dried fruit and nuts in winter) or mix it up, as I've done here. (Pictured on pages 38–39.)

150 g/5½ oz. medium hard cheese, such as Cheddar or Manchego

150 g/5½ oz. soft, mild and creamy cheese, such as Brie

150 g/5½ oz. medium soft cheese, such as a goat's cheese

150 g/5½ oz. any medium strength blue cheese

100 g/⅓ cup store-bought caramelized onion chutney (or Fennel Seed and Whiskey Apple Chutney, see right)

100 g/⅓ cup sweet chilli/chili relish

100 g/⅓ cup membrillo/quince jelly

120 g/4½ oz. mixed crackers for cheese

1 small baguette, sliced

a knob/pat of butter

3 fresh figs, halved

1 bunch of red grapes

8 dates

3 stems of on-the-vine cherry or baby plum tomatoes

6 cocktail gherkins/dill pickles

100 g/3½ oz. unsalted mixed nuts

20 g/¾ oz. mixed baby salad leaves

**FOR THE FENNEL SEED AND WHISKEY APPLE CHUTNEY**

1 tbsp fennel seeds

1 tsp coriander seeds

3 dessert apples (about 450 g/1 lb.)

45 ml/3 tbsp whiskey

2 red onions, diced

½ bird's eye chilli/chile, sliced

300 g/1½ cups caster/superfine sugar

250 ml/1 cup malt vinegar

60 g/1 cup raisins

½ tsp salt

**MAKES 3 X 385-ML/13½-OZ. JARS**

**PRESENTATION**
*a large circular platter, marble works well as it stays nice and cool. plus a cheese knife or two*

**SERVES 4-6**

For the chutney, lightly toast the fennel and coriander seeds in a dry, heavy-based saucepan for a minute. Remove from the heat and lightly crack the seeds using the base of a cup. Leave the seeds in the pan.

Dice the apples (leave the peel on, but discard the cores) and add to the saucepan, pour in half the whiskey (save the remaining half) and add the remaining ingredients. Bring the mixture to a boil, then reduce the heat to a gentle simmer for 1 hour, stirring occasionally to stop it sticking to the base of the pan. It will thicken slightly but the liquid will remain quite fluid – that's fine as it thickens further once cool. Once the pan is off the heat, stir in the remaining whiskey and pour into sterilized jars seal while still hot, then leave to cool.

**HOW TO ASSEMBLE**
Start by placing the wedges of cheese onto the board with lots of space between them. Spoon the different chutneys and the membrillo near whichever cheese you feel they pair best with.

Fan out a line or two of the crackers and the same with the slices of baguette. Add the knob/pat of butter. Now dot around groups of figs, bunches of grapes, dates, tomatoes, gherkins, nuts and finally the mixed salad leaves to fill in all the spaces.

# WINE BITES SHARER

My wine bites board boasts a gorgeous variety of breads and breadsticks, with mouthwateringly savoury dips to enjoy with a glass of good red wine. Simply buy in the breads, make some classy dips (or buy those in too, if pushed for time) and enjoy with friends. To give the board some texture, cut the bread into different shapes – some cubed, some sliced, some ripped, some left whole with a bread knife on the board for friends to slice their own. Toast a few slices as well. I opt for a variety of flavoured breads, seeded, non-seeded, etc. – buy the best you can afford from your local artisan bakery. (Pictured on pages 42–43.)

a variety of breads, such as olive bread, sundried tomato bread, white pavé and sourdough

8 grissini (breadsticks)

100 g/½ cup salted butter

80 g/3 oz. caperberries

100 g/3½ oz. physalis/cape gooseberries

### GARLIC BREAD

120 g/½ cup plus 1 tbsp salted butter

40 ml/2¾ tbsp olive oil

6 large garlic cloves, crushed

a small bunch of fresh flat-leaf parsley, chopped

1 baguette

a pinch of sea salt

### BAKED BROWN SUGAR AND WALNUT CAMEMBERT

250-g/9-oz. Camembert wheel

1 tsp butter

1 tbsp light brown sugar

6 walnuts, shelled and broken

### BAGNA CAUDA

300 ml/1¼ cups olive oil

12 garlic cloves, crushed

50 g/2 oz. anchovy fillets, drained

30 g/2 tbsp butter

finely grated lemon zest

a few pink peppercorns, cracked

### PRESENTATION
*a large circular platter*

### SERVES 6-8

### GARLIC BREAD

Preheat the oven to 200°C fan/220°C/425°F/Gas 7.

To make the garlic butter, whisk together the butter, half the olive oil, garlic and parsley until you have thick paste. Make incisions into the baguette about 5 cm/2 in. apart (making sure you don't cut all the way through) and spread a tablespoon of the garlic butter into each slit. Continue until you've used up all the garlic butter. Holding the baguette from below so the slits are slightly open, drizzle a fine line of olive oil across the top, letting it fall into the slits, sprinkle sea salt over the top and wrap in foil.

Bake in the preheated oven for 10 minutes or until the baguette is warm and slightly crusty. Leave the garlic bread wrapped in its foil until ready to serve.

### BAKED BROWN SUGAR AND WALNUT CAMEMBERT

Reduce the oven temperature to 180°C fan/200°C/400°F/Gas 6.

Unwrap the cheese from its packaging, discarding any plastic, and place it back into the box. Spread the butter over the cheese, score the top a few times and sprinkle over the brown sugar and walnuts. Bake in the oven for 15–20 minutes or until the cheese is gooey. Place on the board.

### BAGNA CAUDA

Pour the olive oil into a heavy-based pan along with the garlic and heat gently to avoid the garlic burning – you want to cook this slowly. Once the garlic has infused for 3–4 minutes, add the anchovies and keep stirring until they have dissolved. Whisk in the butter and once incorporated remove the pan from the heat. Finish by scattering a little lemon zest and cracked pink peppercorns over the top.

### HOW TO ASSEMBLE

First place the baked camembert and bagna cauda on the board, followed by the knob/pat of butter and the garlic bread, wrapped in foil to keep it warm until ready to serve.

Keep the same types of bread grouped together and place on the board along with the breadsticks, then fill in any gaps with the caperberries and physalis/cape gooseberries. Enjoy with your favourite bottle of wine (or two).

# CHARCUTERIE TRAY

I like my charcuterie boards to be luxurious and generous, a gastronomic indulgence that involves no cooking whatsoever. I allow about 85 g/3 oz. sliced meat per person, but add whole cuts of salami and chorizo on top (mainly as I like to use those leftovers in other recipes or to snack on over the weeks that follow). Try to incorporate variety of textures and flavours with your choice of charcuterie to keep it interesting with little pockets of flavour boosters to complement the cold cuts, like peppery rocket/arugula, on-the-vine tomatoes, baby gherkins/dill pickles and sweet chutneys and relishes. If you include a pâté, add a sliced baguette to your board.

160 g/5½ oz. Serrano ham, sliced

80 g/3 oz. bresaola, thinly sliced

80 g/3 oz. sliced peppercorn salami

80 g/3 oz. honey roast ham, thinly sliced

80 g/3 oz. smoked ham, such as Lonza, or duck breast, thinly sliced

100 g/3½ oz. whole salami

200 g/7 oz. whole cured chorizo ring

150 g/5½ oz. Ardennes-style coarse pâté

100 g/3½ oz. sweet chilli/chili relish (or your preferred choice of chutney)

1 baguette, thinly sliced

a knob/pat of salted butter

100 g/3½ oz. green olives, pitted

50 g/2 oz. cornichons

100 g/3½ oz. on-the-vine piccolo tomatoes

25 g/¾ oz. rocket/arugula

a drizzle of good olive oil

freshly ground black pepper

**PRESENTATION**
*a square wooden tray with shallow sides*

**SERVES 6–8**

## HOW TO ASSEMBLE

Group the pre-sliced meats around the board with space between them. Next, place the whole cuts of salami and chorizo on the board and slice a few very thin slithers off each piece to get the party started. (If you prefer, you can pre-slice these too and just add to the board with the other meats, as pictured.)

Add the pâté to the board, garnish with a dollop of chutney and a few turns of cracked black pepper. Offer more chutney in a ramekin on the side.

Add a few thin slices of baguette grouped together on the board with the remaining baguette on the side for guests to help themselves later; a little salted butter is always a good idea.

Dot ramekins or small dishes of olives and gherkins/dill pickles in the available spaces, nestle the tomatoes amongst the other ingredients and finish with a few leaves of rocket/arugula to fill the gaps. Add a little drizzle of olive oil over each cluster of leaves.

# 'FRITTO MISTO' PLATTER

Crispy fried fish! One of my favourite sharers and surprisingly easy to make. All the seafood is cooked in the same way, making this relatively simple to put together. The fish listed below is my preferred selection, but adjust the quantities according to the seafood you prefer or can source. As well as the classic squeeze of lemon juice, you need a good sauce to slather over these little crispy bites, such as my lip-smacking 'nduja mayo.

300 g/10½ oz. large squid tubes and tentacles

500 g/1 lb. 2 oz. thick fish fillets, such as cod, hake, pollock

16 king prawns/jumbo shrimp

6–8 scallops, in the shell

100 g/3½ oz. whitebait

6–8 asparagus spears

270 g/2 cups plain/all-purpose flour

100 g/1 cup cornflour/cornstarch

1 tsp cayenne pepper

500 ml/2 cups vegetable oil

2 lemons, cut into wedges

a pinch of mild chilli/chili powder

salt and freshly ground black pepper

**'NDUJA MAYONNAISE**

250 ml/1 cup mayonnaise

3 tbsp 'nduja

a squeeze of lemon juice

**COCKTAIL SAUCE**

125 ml/½ cup tomato ketchup

125 ml/½ cup sriracha sauce

1 tbsp creamed horseradish

2 tsp Worcestershire sauce

a squeeze of lemon juice

**PRESENTATION**

*a rectangular or oval ceramic or metal platter and 2 ramekins or small dishes*

**SERVES 6–8**

First, make the sauces. Whisk all the ingredients for each one together, then taste and adjust accordingly, adding more of any of the ingredients to suit your preference. Once done, decant the sauces into ramekins and set aside.

**PREPARE THE SEAFOOD AND ASPARAGUS, AS FOLLOWS:**

Cut the squid into 2.5-cm/1-in. rings and leave the tentacles whole. Cut the fish into 3-cm/1¼-in. chunks. Peel the prawns/shrimp, leaving the tail on. To devein them simply score along the length of its back and peel out the dark vein. For the scallops, remove the meat and roe from the shell, clean the shells thoroughly and set aside for later. Rinse the whitebait under cold running water. Snap off any woody ends from the asparagus spears, if necessary.

Mix the flour, cornflour/cornstarch and cayenne together in a bowl, season very generously with salt and pepper.

Heat the vegetable oil in a heavy-based saucepan. Once shimmering (to the point a piece of bread dropped in sizzles immediately but doesn't burn) you are ready to start cooking.

The cooking method is the same for each ingredient with only the cooking time varying. Keep the groups of ingredients together (i.e. cook all the whitebait together).

Dredge each ingredient in the seasoned flour until well coated, shake off any excess flour, then fry in batches in the hot oil turning them over halfway through the cooking times below.

**Fish fillets:** 4 minutes

**Whitebait, scallops and prawns/shrimp:** 2 minutes

**Squid and asparagus:** 1 minute

Once you've cooked each batch, place onto paper towels to drain and season immediately with salt.

## HOW TO ASSEMBLE

Place the scallop shells in groups on the platter with one scallop back into each shell (if space is tight, put three scallops in each shell).

Position the sauces on the platter then load it with batches of fried fish (it doesn't have to be too neat). Once done, nestle the asparagus in a couple of spots and fill any remaining gaps with lemon wedges. Add a final seasoning of salt and a pinch of mild chilli/chili powder. Serve whilst hot.

# BBQ SKEWERS BOARD

Given my Greek Cypriot heritage, I couldn't really write a book without including a few kebab/kabob-style skewers could I? Cook these tasty morsels on the barbecue/outdoor grill in summer, or in a stovetop griddle pan any time of the year for an instant taste of summer. (Pictured on pages 50–51.)

12 flour tortilla wraps

1 red onion, thinly sliced

1 cucumber, sliced

1 buffalo (steak) tomato, sliced

½ iceberg lettuce, cut into wedges

a handful each of fresh flat-leaf parsley and fresh coriander/cilantro, torn

1 lemon and 1 lime, halved and griddled

### CHIMICHURRI DRESSING

1 garlic clove, crushed

leaves from a few sprigs each of fresh flat-leaf parsley and coriander/cilantro, chopped

1 tbsp dried oregano

½ fresh red chilli/chile

1 small ripe tomato

½ tsp salt

freshly squeezed juice of ½ lemon

4 tbsp olive oil

1 tbsp red wine vinegar

### ASIAN GLAZE

4 tbsp soy sauce

2 tbsp tomato purée/paste

½ tbsp runny honey

1 tsp red wine vinegar

1 stick lemongrass, crushed and finely chopped

2.5-cm/1-in. piece of fresh ginger, finely grated

1 garlic clove, crushed

a pinch of salt

### RAITA

250 g/1 cup natural/plain Greek yogurt

½ tsp ground cumin

½ tsp garam masala

a pinch of salt

½ garlic clove, crushed

### SOUTH AMERICAN STEAK SKEWERS

500 g/1 lb. 2 oz. thick cut rump steak, cut into 2.5-cm/1-in. cubes

2 red onions, cut into eighths

### ASIAN PRAWN SKEWERS

12 king prawns/jumbo shrimp, shell on, deveined (see page 48), underside butterflied

1 lime, cut into wedges

### VEGETABLE PANEER SKEWERS

200 g/7 oz. paneer, cut into 2.5-cm/1-in. cubes

2 courgettes/zucchini, cut into 2.5-cm/1-in. chunks

1 red onion, cut into eighths

½ head cauliflower, broken into florets

1 tbsp curry powder

2 tbsp olive oil

### PRESENTATION
*a very large, oiled wooden board or a metal tray both work here*

### SERVES 4–6

If using wooden skewers, soak in water for 30 minutes before use. Preheat your barbecue/outdoor grill if using.

## CHIMICHURRI DRESSING

Blend all the ingredients together in a food processor or pestle and mortar to make a loose dressing; add more oil or vinegar as needed.

## ASIAN GLAZE

Mix all the ingredients together in a small bowl, then set aside.

## RAITA

Mix all the raita ingredients together in a small serving bowl, then chill until ready to serve.

## SOUTH AMERICAN STEAK SKEWERS

Thread the chunks of steak and red onion onto skewers, continuing until all the steak is used; try to have at least five chunks of steak per skewer. Before cooking, drizzle the skewers with a little of the chimichurri dressing and use a brush to spread it over the meat. (You'll be serving left over sauce so don't dip the brush that has touched the raw meat into the sauce.) Cook the skewers on a preheated barbecue/outdoor grill·or hot griddle pan for 2–3 minutes on each side. Set aside and keep warm.

## ASIAN PRAWN/SHRIMP SKEWERS

Devein the prawns/shrimp following the instructions on page 48. Thread a wedge of lime onto each skewer and spear a prawn/shrimp lengthways onto the skewer (piercing through the flesh side of the tail first, then back up through the flesh near the head end), finally add another piece of lime. Depending how big the prawns/shrimp are, thread one or two per skewer. Again, drizzle and then lightly brush over some of the Asian glaze (without double-dipping!), pouring the remaining dressing into a dipping bowl for later.

Cook the skewers on a preheated barbecue/outdoor grill or hot griddle pan for 2 minutes on each side, then set aside and keep warm.

## VEGETABLE PANEER SKEWERS

Thread all the chunks of cheese and vegetables alternately onto the skewers until you have used them all. Mix the curry powder into the olive oil and brush over the skewers. Cook the skewers on a preheated barbecue/outdoor grill or hot griddle pan for 3–4 minutes on each side, then set aside and keep warm.

## HOW TO ASSEMBLE

Place the tortilla wraps overlapping at one end of the board. Group the skewers together on the board (alternatively, place the skewers on top of the tortillas so they catch all juices).

Dot the two different dressings and raita in their bowls around the board and add the griddled halves of lime and lemon. Fill all the gaps with the remaining board ingredients, again keeping them grouped together and framed on the board.

# BESPOKE BURGER BOARD

I'm a huge fan of a good burger and this build-your-own burger board is a great way to serve them up for a group of family or friends, with everyone creating their own burger. It's best to place everything on the board and then, as the burgers are cooked, add them at the last minute so that they are still hot.

150 g/¾ cup tomato ketchup

150 g/¾ cup mayonnaise

150 g/¾ cup burger relish

2 Little Gem/Boston lettuces or 1 Cos/Romaine lettuce, leaves separated

2 buffalo (steak) tomatoes, thinly sliced

2 red onions, thinly sliced into rings

8 brioche or sesame burger buns, or a mix of the two

100 g/3½ oz. gherkins/dill pickles, sliced

1 avocado, stoned/pitted, peeled and sliced

100 g/3½ oz. crispy fried onions

12 rashers/slices smoked streaky bacon

1 tbsp olive oil, plus extra for oiling the burger and frying

1 kg/2 lb. 4 oz. minced/ground steak (or 8 good-quality ready-made beef patties)

1 tsp salt

freshly ground black pepper

8 slices burger cheese

225 g/8 oz. halloumi, sliced 1-cm/½-in. thick

4 Portobello mushrooms, stalks trimmed

PRESENTATION
*a very large wooden board*

SERVES 4-6

### HOW TO ASSEMBLE

Build the board first, leaving space for the burgers, mushrooms and halloumi as you will be adding these last. Decant the condiments (ketchup, mayo and burger relish) into ramekins or small bowls and place on the board. Next, place the rest of the ingredients together on the board keeping them in groups. (If you are doing this in advance, sprinkle the avocado with a little lemon juice to prevent it from discolouring.) When the board is set up, start cooking the bacon, burgers, mushrooms and halloumi. If you wish, toast the cut sides of the burger buns.

### BACON

Fry the bacon in a very hot pan with 1 tablespoon of oil for 3-4 minutes until crisp, turning halfway. Drain on paper towels and add to the board.

### BURGERS

Take the minced/ground steak out of the fridge 30 minutes before cooking to bring it to room temperature. Tip the steak into a large bowl, season with 1 teaspoon of salt and some black pepper and incorporate with your hands, but don't overwork the mixture. Divide equally into 8 balls, then flatten into a pattie (about 1 cm/¾ in. thick). Lightly oil each pattie, then place into a hot frying pan/skillet. Leave to cook without moving them for 4 minutes, then turn over and cook for another 4 minutes on the the other side for medium-well done. Add 1 tablespoon of water to the pan, cover with a lid and cook for 1 further minute. If you want melted cheese on top, add the cheese to the pattie just before covering with the lid (alternatively, add the cheese slices to the board). Cook the patties in batches, loading the board as you go along. If using shop-bought patties, cook according to the package instructions.

### HALLOUMI AND MUSHROOMS

Season the halloumi slices with freshly ground black pepper. In a very hot pan, add a splash of olive oil and fry the halloumi and mushrooms for 1 minute on each side and place directly onto the board.

# SUNDAY ROAST SHARER

There's nothing like gathering around to share a roast dinner on a Sunday - something of a British tradition. I've played with all the key elements so you can serve them on a board as a fun centrepiece. The super-sized Yorkshire puds/popovers act as edible serving bowls here. Clever, huh?

2 kg/4½ lb. rib of beef, bone in

a few sprigs of fresh rosemary

a few sprigs of fresh thyme

4 tbsp Dijon mustard

3 onions, halved

1 garlic bulb, halved horizontally

500 g/1 lb. 2 oz. heritage carrots, peeled

1 tbsp cornflour/cornstarch

1 kg/2 lb. 4 oz. new/baby potatoes

500 g/1 lb. 2 oz. greens, sliced

300 g/2 cups frozen petits pois

4 tbsp vegetable oil

a knob/pat of butter

100 g/3½ oz. creamed horseradish

sea salt and freshly ground black pepper

**YORKSHIRE PUDDINGS/ POPOVERS**

260 g/2 cups plain/ all-purpose flour

500 ml/2 cups whole/full-fat milk

4 large eggs

a pinch of salt and freshly ground black pepper

vegetable oil

**PRESENTATION**
*a large slate board*

**SERVES 4-6**

After the beef is cooked and resting out of the oven, the potatoes and Yorkshire puddings/popovers can be put into the oven at the same time.

Preheat the oven to 220°C fan/240°C/475°F/Gas 9.

**RIB OF BEEF**

Take the beef out of the fridge 1 hour before cooking to bring it to room temperature. Place it in a roasting pan. Chop the rosemary and thyme leaves and mix with the mustard, season with 1 teaspoon of salt and cracked black pepper and spoon over the meat. Add the onions, garlic and carrots to the roasting pan. Roast the beef for 20 minutes at 220°C fan/240°C/475°F/Gas 9, then reduce the oven temperature to 160°C fan/180°C/350°F/Gas 4 for a further 1 hour. Remove the roasting pan from the oven, cover loosely with foil and let the meat rest for 30 minutes before carving.

**MINI ROASTIES**

Preheat the oven to 200°C fan/220°C/425°F/Gas 7.

Boil the new/baby potatoes in a saucepan of water for 12 minutes or until tender, drain and leave to steam dry. Place the boiled potatoes on a baking sheet and crack each one with the back of a fork. Drizzle a little olive oil over the potatoes and season with salt and pepper. When the Yorkshire puddings/popovers are ready to go in the oven, pop in the potatoes for 30 minutes or until they are crispy.

**YORKSHIRE PUDDINGS/POPOVERS**

While the potatoes are boiling, mix all the Yorkshire pudding/popover ingredients together in a bowl and set aside. Pour enough oil into two heavy-based ovenproof 25-cm/10-in. pans to cover their bases and heat on the stovetop. When the oil sizzles (and is still on the heat), pour the batter into the two pans and once it sizzles immediately place both pans, along with the prepared potatoes – into the preheated oven for 30 minutes – don't open the oven door until the end of the cooking time as the puddings/popovers may sink!

### GREENS AND PEAS

Fry the shredded greens in a heavy-based pan with a little olive oil for a few minutes on a high heat, then fold in the petits pois. After a couple of minutes, add a splash of water and immediately cover the pan with a lid. Cook covered for 3 minutes on a high heat, then remove the lid and leave the water to evaporate. Remove from the heat, stir in a knob/pat of butter and season generously with salt and pepper.

### GRAVY

To make the gravy, mix the cornflour/cornstarch with 2 tablespoons of cold water to make a slurry. Pour the juices from the roasting pan into a saucepan, skim off any fat and pour in the cornflour/cornstarch slurry, adding more water if you need more gravy. Heat gently, stirring until thick, then decant into a serving jug/pitcher.

### HOW TO ASSEMBLE

Place both Yorkshire puddings/popovers onto the board. Fill one with cooked greens, peas, carrots and onions. Carve the beef and fill the second one with sliced meat. Squeeze the gravy jug/pitcher onto the board along with the creamed horseradish in a couple of ramekins or small bowls and the roasted potatoes and garlic dotted around the board in clusters.

# CHAPTER
## 3
# Big Nights In

# KITCHEN DISCO CANAPÉS

It's so kitsch it's cool! My retro-inspired kitchen disco canapé board is a throwback that's making a comeback! I've worked up a few simple fingerfood recipes (including my mum's famous Scotch egg recipe!), but if you prefer, you can buy some of it in and concentrate on hanging that glitter ball in the kitchen and shaking up some '70s cocktails!

1 large grapefruit, ¼ sliced off for a flat surface, to use as a base for the skewers

24 ready-made vol-au-vent cases (see recipes for fillings, use 8 cases for each filling)

### SCOTCH EGGS

500 g/1 lb. 2 oz. sausagemeat

6 eggs, 5 for inside the Scotch eggs and 1 beaten

250 g/2 cups golden dried breadcrumbs

1 tbsp chilli/chili powder

salt and freshly ground black pepper

### HAM AND CHEESE SLIDERS

20 g/1½ tbsp butter, melted

4 tsp runny honey, plus a few extra drops

1 tbsp freshly chopped flat-leaf parsley

a pinch of sea salt

2 tsp Dijon mustard

8 mini burger buns or rolls

8 Cheddar slices

8 ham slices

8 firm mozzarella slices

### CARIBBEAN PINEAPPLE AND CHEESE SKEWERS

150 g/5½ oz. semi-hard goat's cheese

100 g/1⅓ cups dessicated/dried shredded coconut

a pinch of chilli/hot red pepper flakes

200 g/7 oz. pineapple, cut into bite-size wedges or cubes

1 tbsp brown sugar

20 g/1½ tbsp butter

2 tbsp dark rum

### PESTO MOZZARELLA SKEWERS

50 g/⅜ cup pine nuts

100 g/3½ oz. mini mozzarella balls

100 g/½ cup green pesto

8 cherry tomatoes

8 basil leaves

### TAPAS SKEWERS

100 g/3½ oz. Manchego

50 g/2 oz. chorizo slices

12 rocket/arugula leaves

12 pitted green olives

### BROWN BUTTER WILD MUSHROOM VOL-AU-VENTS

20 g/1½ tbsp butter

100 g/3½ oz. wild mushrooms

3 tbsp sweet sherry

2 tbsp double/heavy cream

a pinch of salt

½ tsp freshly squeezed lemon juice

8 small stalks of fresh thyme

### CRAYFISH COCKTAIL VOL-AU-VENTS

80 g/3 oz. cooked crayfish tails

a few sprigs of fresh dill, to garnish

a pinch of sweet paprika, to garnish

For the cocktail sauce:

3 tbsp tomato ketchup

4 tbsp mayonnaise

½ tsp Worcestershire sauce

½ tsp hot sauce

½ tsp freshly squeezed lemon juice

salt and freshly ground black pepper

### ASPARAGUS AND QUAIL'S EGG VOL-AU-VENTS

12 asparagus spears, halved lengthways

4 quail's eggs

4 chives, cut into 5-cm/2-in. strips

freshly ground black pepper

For the Hollandaise sauce:

3 eggs

1 tbsp freshly squeezed lemon juice

a pinch of cayenne pepper

100 g/7 tbsp salted butter

### PRESENTATION
*a large circular platter and a selection of wooden or bamboo olive picks or short skewers*

### SERVES 6-8

### SCOTCH EGGS

Preheat the oven to 170°C fan/190°C/375°F/Gas 5.

Bring a saucepan of water to a boil. Add the eggs and cook for 4 minutes, then remove the pan from the heat and leave the eggs to sit in the water for a further 4 minutes. Remove, rinse under cold running water, peel, and reserve.

Mix the breadcrumbs in a shallow bowl with the chilli/chili powder and salt and pepper.

Divide the sausagemeat into 5 equal portions and roll each one into a ball. Use your thumb to make an indent and widen the cavity until it is large enough to place one of the boiled eggs in the middle, then evenly wrap the sausagemeat around the egg. Dip the covered Scotch egg into the beaten egg, then roll it in the breadcrumbs, ensuring it is fully coated. Continue until all the eggs are coated, then place on a baking sheet lined with parchment paper.

Bake in the preheated oven for 25 minutes or until the breadcrumbs are golden. Eat hot or cold, but always with mustard!

### HAM AND CHEESE SLIDERS

Preheat the oven to 180°C fan/200°C/400°F/Gas 6.

Mix the melted butter with the parsley, a few drops of honey and a pinch of sea salt and set aside.

Mix the honey and mustard together and set aside.

Lay the bottom half of the buns in an ovenproof frying pan or skillet so they fit snugly. Lay a slice of Cheddar, then ham, then mozzarella on each bun. Swipe a layer of the honey mustard on the inside of the bun tops and place on top.

Cover the pan with foil and bake in the preheated oven for 20 minutes. Brush the bun tops with the melted butter mixture and return to the oven for 5 minutes.

### CARIBBEAN PINEAPPLE AND CHEESE SKEWERS

Slice the goat's cheese into 1-cm/½-in. chunks and gently roll into balls, then roll in the coconut-chilli mix until well coated. Place in the fridge to harden (this makes them easier to skewer).

Toast the coconut in a dry frying pan or skillet until it turns golden, then remove into a bowl and add the chilli/hot red pepper flakes. Set aside.

Dust the pineapple cubes with brown sugar and heat the butter in a frying pan or skillet. Once foaming, place the pineapple cubes in the pan for 1 minute on each side, just long enough for them to caramelize, then turn the heat up to high, pour in the rum and swirl around, spooning it over the pineapple until almost fully reduced. Remove from the heat and set aside.

Thread a ball of goat's cheese onto each skewer, then a cube of pineapple. Continue until all the cheese balls and pineapple are used up. Insert the skewers into the grapefruit, which acts as a base.

### PESTO MOZZARELLA SKEWERS

Tip the pine nuts onto a flat plate.

Roll the mozzarella balls in the pesto until well covered. Thread a cherry tomato onto each skewer, then a mozzarella ball, then a basil leaf (if large, fold in half). Roll each skewer in pine nuts. The mozzarella balls won't be covered in pine nuts, but a few is enough to give it some crunch. Insert the skewers into the grapefruit.

### TAPAS SKEWERS

Cut the Manchego into small wedges and thread onto skewers. Fold the chorizo slices into four to make a wedge shape, then thread onto the skewers, followed by a few rocket/arugula leaves rolled together. Finish each skewer with an olive and then place in the grapefruit.

## VOL-AU-VENTS

Cook the vol-au-vent cases according to the package instructions. Fill with the following recipes.

## BROWN BUTTER WILD MUSHROOM VOL-AU-VENTS

Heat the butter in heavy-based pan over a high heat for a few minutes until it foams and starts to turn brown, then scatter in the mushrooms with a few thyme leaves and don't move them. After a minute, give them a quick stir and add the sherry. Reduce by half, then remove from the heat and pour in the cream with a pinch of salt and few drops of lemon juice. Fill each vol-au-vent case with the mushroom mixture, give them a turn of black pepper and spear with a thyme stalk to garnish.

## CRAYFISH COCKTAIL VOL-AU-VENTS

Mix all the cocktail sauce ingredients together, then fold in the crayfish. Once ready to serve, fill each vol-au-vent case with the crayfish cocktail mixture and garnish with a sprig of dill and a pinch of paprika for colour.

## ASPARAGUS AND QUAIL'S EGG VOL-AU-VENTS

Start with the Hollandaise sauce. Add two egg yolks and one whole egg to a blender along with the lemon juice and cayenne pepper, then blitz for a few seconds. Melt the butter in small saucepan and leave to cool for a minute. Pour it into a bowl to help it cool slightly and pour the lot (while still warm) into the blender and very quickly blend for 1 minute – you will have a luxurious sauce. Taste and add more lemon juice if needed and set aside.

Bring a saucepan of water to a boil. Carefully add the quail's eggs and cook for 2 minutes. Remove from the pan and cool under cold running water. Once cool enough to handle, carefully peel the eggs and use a sharp knife to cut in half. Season with cracked black pepper.

Bring a saucepan of water to a boil. Drop the asparagus spears in for 30 seconds and remove with a slotted spoon into iced water; just enough to bring their colour out.

Half-fill each vol-au-vent case with the Hollandaise sauce, top with a quail's egg, then spear three halved asparagus tips and chives behind the eggs so they protrude by 2.5 cm/1 in. Add a dusting of cayenne pepper, if you wish.

## HOW TO ASSEMBLE

Place the grapefruit with skewers proudly on the board. Add the sliders. Group the Scotch eggs together, cutting them in half to show off the runny yolks and swipe a dollop of mustard next to them. Dot the vol-au-vents around the board in groups and finish by filling any gaps with any remaining ingredients (olives, mozzarella balls, rocket/arugula leaves, etc.). To serve, get your dancing shoes on and shake up some retro cocktails!

# CARPET PICNIC BOARD

Carpet picnic?! What is this madness I hear you cry! This board is all about the convenience of picnicking in the warmth and comfort of your own home. All the food fun, without having to check the weather forecast, or risk being assailed by wasps in the great outdoors. You can buy in most of these ingredients or choose to make your own with my recipes below. The hummus and crudités are an optional addition, but do constitute one of your five a day! (Pictured on pages 66–67.)

200 g/7½ oz. plain tortilla chips

200 g/7½ oz. your favourite hummus (I've gone with beetroot/beet here)

4 Scotch eggs (store-bought or see recipe on pages 62–63)

mustard, to serve

chunky pickle, to serve

a selection carrots, celery, cucumber, red (bell) pepper, cut into crudités batons and a handful of cherry tomatoes (all optional)

**FENNEL SEED SAUSAGE ROLLS**

2 tbsp fennel seeds

500 g/1 lb. 2 oz. sausagemeat

400 g/14 oz. ready-made puff pastry dough

50 g/6 tbsp plain/all-purpose flour, for dusting

1 egg, beaten

1 tbsp nigella seeds

**TOMATO SALSA**

12 cherry tomatoes

1 garlic clove

¼ tsp salt

1 bird's eye chilli/chile

3 tbsp olive oil

a few sprigs of fresh coriander/cilantro, chopped

1 tbsp cider vinegar

**PASTRAMI AND CHEESE SANDWICHES**

4 tbsp mayonnaise

4 slices thick-cut bread, buttered

4 lettuce leaves

1 on-the-vine vine tomato, sliced

4 slices Cheddar or Monteray Jack

1 large gherkin/dill pickle, thinly sliced

200 g/7½ oz. pastrami

4 tbsp Dijon mustard

**PRESENTATION**
*a large rectangular wooden board, 2 small bowls for dips and cocktail sticks for the sandwiches (optional)*

**SERVES 4-6**

**FENNEL SEED SAUSAGE ROLLS**
Preheat the oven to 180°C fan/200°C/400°F/Gas 6.

Toast the fennel seeds in a dry frying pan or skillet for a minute then crush in a pestle and mortar or with a rolling pin. Mix the crushed seeds into the sausagemeat.

Lightly dust a worksurface with the flour, then roll out the puff pastry into 4 rectangles about 30 x 15 cm/12 x 6 in. and 3 mm/⅛ in. thick.

Take a quarter of the sausagemeat, roll into a sausage shape the same length as the pastry and place on one side of the pastry sheet, 2.5 cm/1 in. in from the edge. Brush the edge of the pastry with beaten egg and fold the pastry over the sausagement filling, pressing down the edges to help it stick together. Repeat to make a total of 4 large sausage rolls.

Scatter the nigella seeds over the sausage rolls and place on a non-stick baking sheet or on a baking sheet lined with parchment paper. Bake in the preheated oven for 30 minutes, or until golden and cooked through.

**TOMATO SALSA**
Add the tomatoes, garlic, salt and chilli/chile to a spice grinder (or use a stick/immersion blender) and pulse to a semi-smooth pulp. Whisk in the olive oil and coriander/cilantro, then add the vinegar in stages, tasting as you go. Spoon into a small serving bowl.

### PASTRAMI AND CHEESE SANDWICHES

Swipe the mayonnaise over the two bottom slices of bread, then
top with lettuce leaves. Layer up slices of tomato, then cheese, then
gherkins/dill pickles, then pastrami and finally spoon the Dijon mustard
over the top slices of bread and place on top to make the sandwiches.
Use a serrated-edge knife to cut sandwiches in half and pierce each
half with cocktail stick to hold together, if liked.

### HOW TO ASSEMBLE

Position the bowl of tomato salsa on the board with the tortilla chips
fanned out around it. Add the bowl of hummus. Group together the
sandwiches, followed by the Scotch eggs with a ramekin of mustard
alongside. Position the sausage rolls on the board (slice one of them),
with the pickle nearby. Finally, fill in the gaps with the crudités, if using.

# MOVIE NIGHT GRAZER

We love a family movie night in our house – we like to spend the first half an hour arguing over what to watch, followed by another half an hour discussing what snacks to break into. My movie night grazer should please everyone and save you a little time... I've included a recipe for my lipsmacking cheese-puff nacho sauce – you can thank me after the film!

180-g/6½-oz. packet plain or flavoured tortilla chips

100-g/3½-oz. packet of mixed root vegetable crisps/chips

180-g/6½-oz. packet salty 'n' sweet popcorn

300 g/10½ oz. tomato salsa (store-bought or see recipe on page 68)

300g /10½ oz. guacamole (store-bought or see recipe on page 91)

50 g/2 oz. sliced jalapeños (from a jar)

80-g/3-oz. packet milk chocolate buttons

### NACHO CHEESE SAUCE

1 tbsp butter

2 tbsp vegetable oil

1 heaped tbsp plain/all-purpose flour

a pinch of ground turmeric (optional, for colour)

250 ml/1 cup whole/full-fat milk

60 g/⅔ cup grated Cheddar

5 slices of burger cheese, torn into pieces

8 g/⅓ oz. (½ a small packet) cheese puffs, crumbled

1–2 tsp pickling juice from the jalapeños

a pinch of salt

### PRESENTATION
*a large circular metal tray with shallow sides and 3 small bowls for dips*

**SERVES 4–6**

### NACHO CHEESE SAUCE
Melt the butter with the oil in a small saucepan, stir in flour and turmeric and cook for 1 minute, then remove the pan from the heat. Pour in all the milk, return to the heat and whisk continuously until bubbling, then remove from the heat.

Whisk in the two cheeses and crumble in the cheese puffs. Return to a low heat, whisking until everything is melted and the sauce is smooth. Finally, season with pinch of salt and teaspoons of the jalapeño pickling juice, which helps to cut through the richness. Leave in the pan ready to warm up just before you are about to serve.

### HOW TO ASSEMBLE
Warm up the nacho cheese sauce just before serving.

Decant the salsa, warm cheese sauce and guacamole into small dipping bowls and place onto the tray. Pile the tortilla chips around the dips. Scatter over the sliced jalapeños.

Add clusters of the vegetable crisps/chips to the tray, along with the popcorn and chocolate buttons. Finish by drizzling the cheese sauce over the tortillas. Settle down on the sofa and get ready to graze!

# GAME-NIGHT
# WINGS 'N' DIPS TRAY

Get ready for game-night! This board is inspired by my memories of sinking a few too many cold beers in my neighbourhood bar when I lived in New Jersey, watching the football and eating more chicken wings than I care to remember! (If you've got vegetarians who want to get in on the game, literally, look out for ready-made jackfruit 'wings' in supermarkets.)

## HOT WINGS AND ONION RINGS

200 g/1½ cups plain/all-purpose flour

50 g/½ cup cornflour/cornstarch

1 tsp salt

1 tsp freshly ground black pepper

1 tbsp cayenne pepper

1 egg

250 ml/1 cup whole/full-fat milk

2 kg/4½ lb. chicken wings

250 ml/1 cup vegetable oil

2 large white onions

## BUFFALO HOT SAUCE

150 ml/⅔ cup hot sauce

1 tbsp honey

1 tsp white wine vinegar

75 g/5 tbsp butter

a pinch of salt

a pinch of cayenne pepper (optional)

## ACCOMPANIMENTS

200 g/7 oz. blue cheese dip

200 g/7 oz. ranch dip

125 ml/½ cup barbecue sauce

celery sticks/ribs, carrot batons and cucumber sticks

2 spring onions/scallions

## BUFFALO HOT SAUCE

In a small saucepan combine the hot sauce, honey, vinegar and butter and heat gently until the butter has melted. Whisk continuously until all the butter is incorporated, then season with a pinch of salt. Add more honey or hot sauce to taste. If you want an extra kick, add a pinch of cayenne pepper. Set aside. Store any leftover hot sauce in a sterilized jar in the fridge after using.

## HOT WINGS AND ONION RINGS

Preheat the oven to 180°C fan/200°C/400°F/Gas 6.

Mix the flours, salt, pepper and cayenne pepper together in a large mixing bowl. In a separate bowl, whisk the egg with the milk.

Joint the chicken wings into three (you can save the tips to make a nice broth).

Drop the wings in the milk mixture first, shake off the excess and drop a handful at a time into the bowl of flour.

In a large heavy-based frying pan or skillet heat the oil until a pinch of flour immediately sizzles but isn't smoking. Carefully place a single layer of wings in the pan (you might have to cook them in batches) and fry the wings for 10 minutes, turning once halfway through cooking. Place the wings onto a wire rack set on a baking sheet and bake in the preheated oven for 8 minutes to finish cooking. Season with pinch of salt once cooked.

Peel and thinly slice the onions into rings. Cook them in the same way as the chicken wings – drop them into the egg mixture, then the flour, then fry for a few minutes until golden and crisp; leave to drain on paper towels.

**PRESENTATION**
*a large rectangular metal tray with shallow sides*

**SERVES 6**

**HOW TO ASSEMBLE**

Divide the wings into three portions; keep one plain with just a sprinkle of salt and pile onto the board. Mix one portion with the barbecue sauce and the final portion with the hot sauce (by placing the wings and sauce together in a bowl and tossing until they are fully coated). Pile the wings on the board in groups.

Dot portions of the onion rings around the board. Decant the ranch and blue cheese dips into ramekins or small bowls and place on the board. Nestle the celery sticks/ribs, carrot batons and cucumber sticks in any gaps. Thinly slice the spring onions/scallions and scatter over the top. Stick a few cold beers on the side, sit back and get ready for the game!

NOTE: For a simplified method, you can cook the hot wings in the oven. Joint the wings, pat them dry with paper towels and season with salt and 1 tablespoon baking powder. Arrange on a baking sheet and bake in an oven preheated to 180°C fan/200°C/400°F/Gas 6 for 30 minutes, turning halfway through the cooking time. They won't be as crispy as the fried ones, but just as tasty!

# DATE-NIGHT DECADENCE

Love is in the air with our date-night board. This board is all about sharing tactile finger food that you can pick up and enjoy with a glass of chilled Champagne. I've purposely kept this light to avoid anyone falling asleep from eating too much – it is date night after all! (Pictured on pages 76–77.)

100 g/½ cup rock salt

4 fresh oysters, opened

1 tbsp hot sauce

2 figs, halved

sourdough bread, toasted and cut into soldiers/strips

### CHOCOLATE-DIPPED STRAWBERRIES

100 g/3½ oz. dark/bittersweet chocolate (70% cocoa)

1 tbsp whole/full-fat milk

10 plump, ripe fresh strawberries, calyxes left on

### LOBSTER TAILS

2 tbsp butter

1 large garlic clove, crushed

½ tsp salt

a few sprigs of fresh flat-leaf parsley, chopped

2 lobster tails (about 100 g/3½ oz. each)

### SUN-DRIED TOMATO DIP

50 g/3 tbsp mayonnaise

30 g/2 tbsp sun-dried tomato paste (or pesto)

1 tsp freshly squeezed lemon juice

a pinch of cayenne pepper

a pinch of sea salt

### ASPARAGUS SPEARS

1 tbsp butter

12 asparagus spears

1 tsp freshly squeezed lemon juice

salt and freshly ground black pepper

### HONEYDEW MELON

½ tsp sea salt

a pinch of cayenne pepper

5 thin slices honeydew melon, skin on and chilled

### PRESENTATION

*a large marble or slate circular platter*

### SERVES 2

### CHOCOLATE-DIPPED STRAWBERRIES

Break the chocolate into a bowl, add the milk and microwave for 30 seconds to melt, then mix together. Dip each strawberry halfway into the chocolate and leave to cool and set.

### LOBSTER TAILS

Preheat the oven to 180°C fan/200°C/400°F/Gas 6. Mix the butter, garlic, salt and parsley together and set aside.

Using a sharp knife or kitchen scissors, cut the top of the lobster tail open along the middle but stop just before you reach the fin. Prise open the shell and dislodge the lobster meat, lifting it slightly out of the shell to rest on top. Score down the middle of the meat to butterfly it open slightly. Place the tails on a baking sheet and roast in the preheated oven for 10 minutes (if your lobster tails are larger/smaller, they will take a fraction longer/less to cook). Remove from the oven, smear the garlic butter all over and return to the oven for 1 minute for the butter to melt.

### SUN-DRIED TOMATO DIP

Mix all ingredients together and set aside.

### ASPARAGUS SPEARS

Melt the butter in a pan, add the asparagus and fry for 2 minutes over a high heat, add the lemon juice for last 30 seconds and remove, then season with salt and pepper.

### HONEYDEW MELON

Mix the salt and cayenne together, then use it to lightly season the melon slices.

## HOW TO ASSEMBLE

Start with the savoury; pile the rock salt on one section of the board and rest the opened oysters on the salt. Season each oyster with a few drops of hot sauce.

Fan out the seasoned melon slices.

Lay the asparagus spears together on the board and neatly spoon over some of the sundried tomato sauce. Pour the rest into a small bowl.

Place the lobster tails on the board next to the toasted sourdough. Pour over any remaining garlic butter.

Finally, at one edge of the board group together the chocolate-coated strawberries and figs for something sweet to finish with.

Put the Champagne on ice and line up the Motown playlist, oh yeah...

# BOX-SET BINGE PICKY TRAY

Binging on a box set seems to be the new norm but it still feels naughty watching episode after episode of a series into the small hours in your PJs. I build this 'picky' grazer in a tray with everything nestled together and enjoy it with tea, lots of tea, or for you chocoholics out there perhaps a mug of hot chocolate with a few mini marshmallows floating on top. (Pictured on pages 80–81.)

- 85-g/3 oz. your favourite pick 'n' mix sweets/candies, such as flying saucers, strawberry bonbons, rock hearts, fudge, taffy etc.
- 85-g/3-oz. packet gummy sweets/candies
- 85-g/3-oz. packet mini chocolate eggs
- 85-g/3-oz. packet salted mini pretzels or salty 'n' sweet popcorn
- ½ x 150-g/5½-oz. packet chocolate cookies, such as Oreos
- 8 salted caramel truffle sweets/candies
- 50 g/2 oz. mixed salted nuts
- 50 g/2 oz. mini marshmallows
- 400-ml/14-oz. jar salted caramel sauce (store-bought or recipe below)

## SALTED CARAMEL SAUCE
- 130 g/⅔ cup golden granulated sugar
- 80 g/5½ tbsp butter, at room temperature
- 125 ml/½ cup double/heavy cream, at room temperature
- 1 tsp sea salt flakes

## BEANIE BROWNIES
- 400-g/14-oz. can black beans, drained and rinsed
- a pinch of salt
- 1 tsp vanilla extract
- 80 ml/5½ tbsp vegetable/flavourless oil
- 3 medium eggs
- 30 g/⅓ cup unsweetened cocoa powder, plus extra for dusting
- 60 g/⅔ cup rolled/old-fashioned oats
- 100 g/½ cup soft brown sugar
- 1 tbsp runny honey
- 40 g/¼ cup chocolate chips
- 25 g/¼ cup hazelnuts, chopped

## PRESENTATION
*a large rectangular tray with shallow sides*

**SERVES 4-6**

### SALTED CARAMEL SAUCE

Place the sugar in a heavy-based saucepan, mix with 4 tablespoons of water and bring to a simmer, stirring occasionally. Continue cooking over a medium-low heat for about 10 minutes until the syrup turns a deep caramel colour, then remove the pan from the heat and quickly fold in the butter. Once fully incorporated, whisk in the cream and return to the heat while you stir in the salt. Remove from the heat and pour into a sterilized jar to store.

### BEANIE BROWNIES

Preheat the oven to 180°C fan/200°C/400°F/Gas 6. Line a 15 x 20-cm/6 x 8-in. baking pan with parchment paper.

In a food processor pulse together the black beans, salt, vanilla extract and vegetable oil until smooth, then crack the eggs into the mixture and pulse until incorporated. Next tip the cocoa, oats, sugar and honey into the mixture and pulse again until incorporated. Now fold in the chocolate chips so they are evenly distributed and pour the mixture into the lined baking pan.

Bake in the preheated oven for 18 minutes. Leave to cool completely before cutting into 8 rectangles.

## HOW TO ASSEMBLE

Decant some of the salted caramel sauce into a dipping bowl and place in the middle of your tray. Group the brownies together, followed by the cookies in a couple of areas, before filling the gaps with clusters of the sweets/candies, gummies, mini eggs, pretzels and popcorn. Drizzle some of the warm salted caramel sauce over a few of the brownies. Get ready to nibble!

TIP: If you are serving hot beverages, you can add the mugs to the tray first and build up the picky bits around the mugs, just don't put any chocolate too near the hot cups to avoid a melty mess!

# GRAND-SLAM TREATS

A fun board that celebrates time spent watching the tennis tournaments, and inspired by Wimbledon in particular, where eating strawberries and cream is an important tradition. A store-bought meringue base is topped with a Champagne cream and presented on pistachio 'grass' complete with tennis-ball macarons. Your serve! (Pictured on pages 84–85.)

2 tbsp raspberry jam/jelly

1 large meringue base, store-bought

400 g/14 oz. fresh strawberries, hulled and halved if large

**TENNIS BALL MACARONS**

9 lemon-flavoured macarons, store-bought

1 white icing/frosting pen

**PISTACHIO CRUMB**

75 g/2½ oz. pistachio nuts, shelled

**CHAMPAGNE AND CHANTILLY CREAMS**

600 ml/2½ cups double/heavy cream

6 tbsp icing/confectioner's sugar

90 ml/⅓ cup Champagne, or other sparkling wine

1 tsp vanilla bean paste

**PRESENTATION**
*a large marble board, plus side plates*

**SERVES 4-6**

**TENNIS BALL MACARONS**
Use the icing/frosting pen to draw two semi-circles on each side to look like the markings on tennis balls, as pictured.

**PISTACHIO CRUMB**
Pulse the pistachio nuts to create a fine crumb and set aside. Do not over pulse, you don't want a pistachio cream!

**CHAMPAGNE AND CHANTILLY CREAMS**
Whisk half the cream with half the icing/confectioner's sugar until it starts to foam, then pour in the Champagne and continue whisking until soft peaks form, then set aside. Combine the remaining cream and icing/confectioner's sugar with the vanilla bean paste and whisk until soft peaks form, then set aside.

**HOW TO ASSEMBLE**
Mix together the raspberry jam/jelly with 1 tablespoon of hot water to loosen. Dot a little cream at one end of the board and place the meringue on top (the cream helps to secure the meringue in place), fill the meringue with the Champagne cream, then generously scatter the strawberries over the top. Drizzle over the loosened raspberry jam/jelly.

Spoon the Chantilly cream onto the rest of the board and smooth out the top. Sprinkle the pistachio crumb over the outer half of the cream to create a 'grass' effect. Dot the 'tennis balls' over the 'grass' and serve, with glass of chilled fizz to wash it down with.

# BUILD-YOUR-OWN
# TACO TUESDAY

Who said tacos were just for Tuesdays?! Oh, apparently it's a 'thing'... So, anyway, these are super easy and lots of fun to put together. I like to use minced/ground beef but this recipe works equally as well with turkey, lamb, pork or a plant-based substitute. The Cajun spices give this a quick hit of flavour, but feel free to add more chilli/chili if preferred.

16 taco shells

200 g/7 oz. guacamole (store-bought or see recipe on page 91)

200 g/7 oz. sour cream

200 g/7 oz. tomato salsa (store-bought or see recipe on page 68)

200 g/2 cups grated cheese (mild Cheddar, feta or any hard cheese)

2 limes, quartered

50 g/2 oz. jarred jalapeños

1 red onion, finely sliced

1 Little Gem/Boston lettuce

**TACOS**

1 kg/2 lb. 4 oz. minced/ ground beef

2 onions, diced

2 garlic clove, crushed

1 tbsp olive oil

4 tbsp tomato ketchup

1 tbsp Worcestershire sauce

3 tomatoes, diced

3 tbsp Cajun spice mix

1 tbsp ground cumin

1 tbsp smoked paprika

a pinch of chipotle chilli/hot pepper flakes

salt and freshly ground black pepper

**PRESENTATION**
*a large round wooden board*

**SERVES 8**

**TACOS**

Fry the minced/ground beef, onions and garlic in a splash of oil in a pan over a high heat for 5 minutes until the meat is cooked, then pour away any excess fat.

Stir in the ketchup, Worcestershire sauce, diced tomatoes and all the spices, along with 125 ml/½ cup water and continue cooking for 5 minutes until the liquid has reduced and thickened. Season with salt and pepper, cover and remove from the heat. Add a splash of water if it is too dry, but don't let it get sloppy.

Heat the taco shells according to the package instructions, then keep warm on a plate, covered with a clean tea/dish towel.

**HOW TO ASSEMBLE**

Heat a cast-iron skillet in the oven or on the stovetop, then reheat the beef mixture and pour into the hot skillet. Place this onto your board just before you are ready to assemble.

Lay the taco shells on the board. Decant the guacamole, salsa, refried beans, sour cream and grated cheese into ramekins or small bowls and place around the board.

Separate the leaves of the lettuce and cluster them in groups, spoon the drained jalapeños onto the board and skillet.Scatter the sliced red onion in different spots to give it some colour. Finally, fill the gaps with the limes and coriander/cilantro and serve.

# REFRIED BLACK BEANS

You can of course buy cans and pouches of ready-made refried beans but they will lack the flavour and texture of my recipe here. It's still quick to make as you use canned black beans, by which I mean black 'turtle' beans, the small shiny variety especially popular in Latin American dishes. Refried doesn't mean the beans are cooked twice – the word comes from the Spanish 'refritos', which actually means well-fried.

2 tbsp olive oil

1 small onion, diced

1 garlic clove, crushed

1 tsp tomato purée/paste

1 tsp smoked paprika

1 tsp ground cumin

a pinch of cayenne pepper

400-g/14-oz. can black beans

a sprig of fresh thyme

½ chicken or vegetable stock cube

**MAKES 8 SMALL SERVINGS**

Heat the oil in a large frying pan or skillet, add the onion and fry for 5 minutes until softened, then stir in the garlic, tomato purée/paste and spices and fry for another minute, then pour in the black beans and add the sprig of thyme.

Refill the empty bean can halfway with hot water, add the stock cube, stir and pour into the pan. Simmer for 5 minutes. Use the back of a fork or a potato masher to very gently crush some of the beans (not all of them, just enough to help thicken the dish). Once the beans are thickened, taste and add more seasoning or cayenne pepper to your preference, then decant into a serving dish.

# GUACAMOLE

You can buy a tub of ready-made guacamole if you like, but nothing beats the fresh taste and silky texture of a bowl of freshly made stuff. If you don't want it too garlicky, you can crush a clove and add a little at a time to suit your taste. Ditto the chilli/chile – leave the seeds in if you want it super spicy, discard them if you prefer a milder heat. Any leftovers make a fabulous toast topping, sprinkled with a little crumbled feta.

1 ripe avocado, peeled and stoned

1 garlic clove, crushed

1 ripe tomato, seeds removed, finely chopped

20 g/¾ oz. coriander/cilantro, freshly chopped, plus extra to serve

2 spring onions/scallions, finely sliced

1 red chilli/chile, finely sliced

2 tbsp olive oil

1 tsp cider vinegar

1 tsp sea salt flakes

a squeeze of lime juice

**MAKES 8 SMALL SERVINGS**

Coarsely mash the avocado in a bowl using the back of a fork; you don't want a purée so keep it chunky. Add the garlic, chopped tomato, coriander/cilantro, sliced spring onions/scallions and sliced chilli/chile. Fold together until combined.

Add the olive oil and vinegar and stir to mix and loosen. Taste, adjusting the seasoning with salt and lime juice to suit your preference. Cover tightly and chill until ready to serve to avoid discolouration.

# CAMPFIRE COOK-OUT

I love camping and have cooked some great food on open fires or in a pit, but if we're camping for more than one night in the height of summer, storing food can be tricky. This board is designed to use non-perishable foods that make a great sharing board without the need to keep them cool, and it's a winner flavourwise too. (Pictured on pages 92–93.)

### SKEWERED CORN

2 corn-on-the-cob, sliced into 5-cm/2-in. discs

50 g/3½ tbsp butter

1 tsp Cajun spice mix

a pinch of salt

### HOT DOGS

6 hot dogs

6 hot dog buns

tomato ketchup, American mustard and crispy onions, to serve

### SMOKY BEANS

400-g/14-oz. can baked beans in tomato sauce

1 tsp smoked paprika

a pinch of chilli/chili powder

1 tsp ground cumin

a sprig of fresh rosemary or thyme

### CORNED BEEF HASH

400 g/14 oz. potatoes, diced

1 large onion, sliced

2 tbsp olive oil

a knob/pat of butter

1 garlic clove, chopped

a few sprigs of fresh thyme

1 green chilli/chile, chopped

340-g/12-oz. can corned beef

1 tbsp Worcestershire sauce

½ tsp salt

½ tsp cracked black pepper

4 eggs

a drizzle of sriracha sauce

### S'MORES SKILLET

200 g/7 oz. dark/ bittersweet chocolate (75% cocoa), broken into chunks

100 g/3½ oz. milk chocolate, broken into chunks

200 g/7 oz. giant marshmallows

12 digestive biscuits/ graham crackers

### PRESENTATION

*a large rectangular metal tray with shallow sides and metal skillets*

**SERVES 4-6**

### SKEWERED CORN

Pierce the corn discs with a skewer. (If using wooden skewers, soak them in water for 30 minutes before use to stop them burning.) Roast over the campfire for about 8–10 minutes, turning frequently. Mix the butter with the Cajun spice and slather it all over the cooked corn. Serve with a sprinkle of salt and extra Cajun spice mix.

### HOT DOGS

Thread one skewer through the end of each hot dog, widthways, then repeat at the other end of the hot dogs with a second skewer. Finally thread a third skewer through the middle of each hot dog so they all lie flat, side by side. Prop the 'rack' of dogs up close to the flames of the campfire and cook until charred, turning once. Serve in split hotdog buns with ketchup, mustard and crispy onions.

### SMOKY BEANS

Open the can of beans, stir in the spices and slide in the sprig of rosemary or thyme. Place the can on glowing embers until warmed through, then either serve from the can or decant the beans into a small saucepan.

### CORNED BEEF HASH

Fry the potatoes and onions in olive oil in the skillet on a medium heat over your campfire until cooked, about 10 minutes. Stir in the butter, garlic, thyme leaves (save a little for garnish) and chilli/chile. Cook for a couple of minutes, then add the corned beef,

Worcestershire sauce, season with salt and pepper and cook until piping hot. In a separate pan (or decant the hash onto a plate), add a splash of oil and fry the eggs so they are crispy around the edges and slide on top of the hash. Finish with thyme leaves, any leftover chilli/chile and a drizzle of sriracha sauce.

## S'MORES SKILLET

Warm a skillet over a small fire and drop the chocolate chunks in so they start to melt. Make sure the skillet isn't too hot, or the chocolate with scorch and burn. Top with the marshmallows. Place the skillet close to the fire, turning it as the marshmallows turn golden.

NOTE: You can also make this in a hot pizza oven or your kitchen oven preheated to 230°C fan/250°C/475°F/Gas 9. Simply build the s'mores skillet as instructed above and bake in either oven for 4–5 minutes until the marshmallows are golden and serve.

## HOW TO ASSEMBLE

Place the skillets of corned beef hash and s'mores on the tray with the can or saucepan of baked beans. Add the hot dogs, the corn and ramekins of condiments. Add a few biscuits/crackers to the tray for dunking into the s'mores skillet.

# CHAPTER
# 4
# Around the World

# ANTIPASTI BRUSCHETTA BAR

The flavours of Italy spread out gloriously for your sharing and dining pleasure! This board couldn't be simpler to assemble, especially if you have a good Italian deli to source from. In essence, this board is a small selection of bruschetta to act as a canvas for all the beautiful ingredients. I've kept this vegetarian, but feel free to slip in some Prosciutto or even Italian-sourced canned sardines, if you like.

1 baguette, thinly sliced

1 garlic clove, peeled

125-g/4½-oz. burrata

a few large handfuls of rocket/arugula

2 tsp balsamic vinegar

1 tbsp extra virgin olive oil

a few sprigs of fresh basil

200 g/7 oz. ricotta

3 figs, halved or quartered

1 tbsp runny honey

100 g/1 cup walnut halves, toasted

a pinch of sea salt

150 g/5½ oz. roasted red and/or yellow (bell) peppers, drained

6 caperberries

100 g/3½ oz. Nocellara olives

6 grissini (breadsticks)

150 g/5½ oz. sun-blushed tomatoes, drained

150 g/5½ oz. marinated chargrilled artichokes, drained

100 g/3½ oz. marinated mushrooms, drained

sea salt and freshly ground black pepper

**PRESENTATION**
*a large circular platter, ceramic or glass*

**SERVES 4-6**

To make the bruschetta toasts, griddle the slices of baguette in a hot griddle pan for a few minutes on each side to give them some colour.

**HOW TO ASSEMBLE**
Rub two slices of the bruschetta toasts lightly with the cut side of a garlic clove. Place them onto the board next to each other to make a double-sized bruschetta. Drizzle ½ teaspoon of balsamic vinegar onto the slices, add a little of the rocket/arugula, then top with the burrata. Drizzle a little olive oil and balsamic vinegar over, finishing with a grinding of black pepper and a couple of small basil leaves.

Spoon a generous amount of ricotta over a couple of the remaining bruschetta toasts slices, top with a couple of fig pieces, drizzle over the honey and finish with a few walnut halves and a pinch of sea salt. Add the ricotta figs to the board.

Place a couple more pieces of bruschetta toasts on the board. Make a small bed of more rocket/arugula on the board and top with the roasted peppers. Next, fill in the gaps with the remaining rocket/arugula, figs, caperberries, olives and grissini. Pile the wetter ingredients (the sun-blushed tomatoes, artichokes and mushrooms) in clusters, with some overlapping the spare bruschetta toasts to absorb some of the oil. Finish with sprigs of basil, a drizzle of balsamic vinegar and lightly crumble the remaining walnuts over the top.

Serve with the remaining toasts and ricotta on the side with small glasses of Prosecco (keeping the rest of the bottle nearby and chilled!).

# A TASTE OF THE LEVANT

Evoking the ancient lands, my Levantine-inspired board is full of Middle Eastern and Eastern Mediterranean flavours – some that I grew up with. You can buy in the falafel but once you've tasted homemade you'll never go back! Enjoy this with fresh mint tea. (Pictured on pages 100–101.)

1 Middle Eastern flatbread (Ramazan pidesi) or 4 pita breads grilled and cut into fingers

1 red onion, sliced into thin wedges

1 tbsp sea salt

2 baby cucumbers, halved lengthways

100 g/3½ oz. mixed olives

3 figs, halved (or quartered if large)

1 pomegranate, half seeded, half left intact

100 g/3½ oz. pistachio nuts (in their shells)

8 Medjool dates

## FALAFEL

180 g/1 cup dried chickpeas/garbanzo beans

a small bunch of fresh coriander/cilantro

a small bunch of fresh flat-leaf parsley

1 shallot, chopped

1 garlic clove, chopped

1 tbsp coriander seeds

1 tsp ground coriander

1 tsp cumin seeds

1 tsp ground cumin

1 tsp salt

1 tsp baking powder

50 g/⅜ cup sesame seeds

vegetable oil, for deep frying

## COFFEE DUKKA SPICE MIX

1 tsp fennel seeds

1 tsp coriander seeds

1 tbsp shelled almonds

1 tsp sesame seeds

1 tsp cumin seeds

1 tsp nigella seeds

6 black peppercorns

a pinch of sea salt flakes

½ tsp fine ground coffee

## TAHINI YOGURT

150 g/¾ cup Greek yogurt

1 tbsp freshly squeezed lemon juice

a pinch of salt

1 small garlic clove, crushed

1 tbsp tahini

a pinch of ground cumin

finely chopped flat-leaf parsley

## CHARRED AUBERGINE/EGGPLANT SLICES

4 baby aubergines/eggplants, halved lengthways (or sliced 1-cm/½-in. thick if using large ones)

## TABBOULEH

50 g/generous ¼ cup bulgur wheat

1 tsp tomato purée/paste

½ vegetable stock cube

60 ml/4 tbsp boiling water

a few sprigs of fresh flat-leaf parsley, coriander/cilantro and mint

1 spring onion/scallion, finely sliced

1–2 tbsp pomegranate seeds

salt and freshly ground black pepper

## PRESENTATION
*a large round serving plate or platter*

## SERVES 4-6

## FALAFEL

Soak the chickpeas/garbanzo beans overnight (or ideally for 24 hours) in plenty of water, then drain.

Add the chickpeas/garbanzo beans with all the ingredients, except the sesame seeds and oil, to a food processor and pulse until you have a fine paste. Take a heaped tablespoon of the mixture and roll into a tight ping-pong ball-sized piece, flatten slightly in the palm of your hand and roll in the sesame seeds. If the falafel do not hold together well, refrigerate for an hour, otherwise continue.

Fill a deep heavy-based pan with vegetable oil, to at least 5 cm/2 in. deep. Heat the oil until a piece of falafel mixture when placed in the oil immediately sizzles but doesn't burn. Fry the falafel pieces for a few minutes until they are crisp and deep golden in colour, then remove using a slotted spoon to drain on paper towels.

NOTE: You can cheat and use canned chickpeas/garbanzo beans. If so, add 40 g/heaping ¼ cup plain/all-purpose flour for each 400-g/14-oz. can of chickpeas/garbanzo beans to hold them together. Not quite as good a texture as the real thing but in a falafel emergency they can work!

## COFFEE DUKKA SPICE MIX

Toast everything except the coffee and salt in a dry heavy-based pan for a couple of minutes until you can smell the aroma. Immediately pour the contents into a pestle and mortar or spice grinder along with the salt and bash or pulse to a coarse grain (the almonds will become much more pulverized than the spices). Stir through the coffee and store in an airtight container.

## TAHINI YOGURT

Mix all the ingredients together, adding a splash of water if it thickens too much, but you want it quite thick, pour into a bowl and reserve.

## CHARRED AUBERGINE/EGGPLANT SLICES

Heat a griddle pan to smoking hot and griddle the aubergine/eggplant slices flesh side down for 2 minutes until they come away from the pan without sticking and have gorgeous charred lines across them. Griddle the other side for another minute, then brush with a little olive oil and set aside. (You can buy a jar of charred aubergine/eggplant if preferred.)

## TABBOULEH

Rinse the bulgur wheat then place in a bowl with the tomato purée/paste and vegetable stock cube. Pour over the boiling water, mix and cover. Finely chop the parsley and coriander/cilantro including the stalks, remove the mint leaves from the stalks and chop, reserve to one side. After 12 minutes, fluff the bulgur wheat with a fork and fold through the chopped herbs, spring onion/scallion and a tablespoon or two of pomegranate seeds, season with a pinch of salt and pepper and set aside.

## HOW TO ASSEMBLE

Start by grouping the larger items around the board; spoon the tabbouleh straight onto the board and add the charred aubergines/eggplant slices, the falafel (cutting one in half to show off the green hue) and the flatbread or pita bread in a couple of places.

Spoon the tahini yogurt directly onto the board, drizzling a little olive oil over the top and garnish with a line of dukka across the middle of the yogurt. Cluster the sliced red onions next to little mound of sea salt (for dipping) and add the baby cucumbers. Any remaining areas can be filled with clusters of olives, figs, dates, pomegranates and pistachios.

# GREEK MEZE SPREAD

I couldn't resist including this meze sharing board – a simple collection of dishes that are close to my heart, and can be quickly put together with minimal effort for a delicious feast inspired by summer days spent on a Greek island. See pages 106–107 for some recipes to try.

6 pita breads

280-g/10 oz. can giant beans in tomato sauce (or see recipe on page 106)

200 g/1 cup tzatziki (ready-made or see recipe on page 107)

400-g/14-oz. can stuffed vine leaves (dolmades)

200 g/1 cup hummus

250 g/9 oz. halloumi

1 tbsp sesame seeds

½ red onion, diced

250 g/9 oz. feta

4 baby cucumbers, quartered lengthways

170 g/6 oz. baby plum tomatoes

a few sprigs of fresh mint and dill

250 g/9 oz. Kalamata olives

a pinch of dried oregano

1 tbsp olive oil, plus extra for frying

1 tbsp white wine vinegar

1 Little Gem/Boston lettuce, 8 leaves removed

½ watermelon, sliced into 1-cm/½-in. triangles

2 tbsp runny honey

lemon wedges, to serve

salt and freshly ground black pepper

**PRESENTATION**
*a long, narrow rectangular board and a selection of small bowls*

**SERVES 6–8**

Lightly toast the pita breads under a preheated grill/broiler (or in a toaster), then slice into strips 5 cm/2 in. wide, keep warm wrapped in a tea/dish towel.

**HALLOUMI**
Slice the block of halloumi lengthways into strips 1 cm/½ in. wide. Tip the sesame seeds onto a plate and lightly coat each halloumi strip in seeds. Heat a small splash of olive oil in a frying pan or skillet and fry the coated halloumi strips for a minute on each side until lightly golden, then remove from the pan onto a plate and cover to keep warm.

**GREEK SALAD LETTUCE BOATS**
Place the diced red onion, half the feta, one baby cucumber and 6 baby plum tomatoes in a bowl and fold them together. Add a few chopped mint leaves, 4 chopped olives and a pinch of dried oregano. Set aside until ready to serve. Dress the mixture just before serving with the olive oil and white wine vinegar and season with salt and pepper. Use a slotted spoon to drain off the excess liquid and fill as many lettuce leaves as you can with the feta mixture. Finally, use the liquid in the bottom of the bowl to lightly dress each Greek salad boat.

**HOW TO ASSEMBLE**
Put the giant beans, tzatziki, vine leaves and hummus in small bowls and/or plates. Put the sesame-coated halloumi on a small plate and drizzle the honey over the top. Arrange these around the board.

Place the prepared Greek salad boats in the centre of the board. Follow this with piles of pita bread and watermelon slices, slightly overlapping each other. Fill any gaps with the olives, mint leaves, dill sprigs, cucumber wedges and nestle in the remaining feta with a drizzle of olive oil. Add the lemon wedges to finish.

# GREEK-STYLE GIANT BEANS IN TOMATO SAUCE

These giant baked beans in a rich tomato sauce are popular throughout the Aegean. In my first book *Orexi!* I included the traditional recipe, which involves slow-cooking dried beans for an entire afternoon, but this is a quicker method that will be ready within the hour. Get these on to cook before you start to set up your meze sharer, or cook them well in advance and reheat them on the stovetop in a pan when you are ready to serve.

4 tbsp olive oil, plus extra for drizzling

1 small onion, diced

1 garlic clove, sliced

2 x 400-g/14-oz. cans butter/lima beans, drained and rinsed

250 ml/1 cup passata/strained tomatoes

1 chicken or vegetable stock cube

1 tbsp paprika

1 tbsp tomato purée/paste

a pinch of sugar

a pinch of chilli/hot red pepper flakes

a few sprigs of fresh flat-leaf parsley, chopped, to garnish

**MAKES 2–4 SERVINGS**

Preheat the oven to 180°C fan/200°C/400°C/Gas 6.

Heat the olive oil in a large frying pan or skillet, add the diced onion and fry for 5 minutes until slightly caramelized, then add the garlic and fry for another minute. Pour in the remaining ingredients and an additional 200 ml/¾ cup water. Bring to a simmer.

Once bubbling, pour the mixture into a 12.5 x 20-cm/5 x 8-in. baking pan and cook in the preheated oven for 45 minutes or until the sauce has reduced and thickened.

Remove the baking pan from the oven, leave to cool for 10 minutes, then tip into a serving dish and dress with a drizzle of olive oil and the chopped parsley.

# TZATZIKI

This classic dip is an essential addition to any meze spread, the cooling yogurt and mint cutting through richer flavours and delicious mopped up with warm pita breads. Any leftover can be stored, covered, in the fridge for a few days and makes a great accompaniment to grilled meats and fried food. Serve it with my BBQ Skewers Board (see page 52), instead of the Raita, or even in place of the dips suggested for the Fritto Misto Platter (see page 48–49) for a Greek rather than Italian twist.

½ cucumber

250 g/1 cup plain/natural Greek yogurt

1 garlic clove, crushed

1 tbsp dried mint

2 sprigs of fresh mint, leaves removed and chopped

1 tbsp freshly squeezed lemon juice

1 tbsp olive oil

½ tsp salt

**MAKES 2–4 SERVINGS**

Trim the end from the cucumber, then cut it in half lengthways and scoop out the seeds. Grate the flesh into a sieve/strainer. Use your hands to squeeze as much juice as possible from the grated cucumber, then place the flesh in a bowl.

Add the remaining ingredients and mix well, then taste and add more lemon juice or salt if necessary. Chill until ready to serve.

# SPANISH TAPAS

Tapas are perhaps the ultimate small plates designed to share. You can buy most of these dishes in but nothing compares to homemade versions. I've also given you a recipe for sangria to complete the experience.

1 wholemeal baguette

12 breadsticks

200 g/7 oz. Manzanilla olives

200 g/7 oz. cured chorizo, half sliced

200 g/7 oz. Manchego, cut into thin slices

## PATATAS BRAVAS

500 ml/2 cups vegetable oil, for deep frying

400 g/14 oz. white potatoes, cut into 2.5-cm/1-in. chunks

1 onion, sliced

100 ml/7 tbsp olive oil

2 garlic cloves, cracked

2 sprigs of fresh thyme

½ tbsp smoked paprika

½ tbsp sweet paprika

a generous pinch of cayenne pepper

1 tsp runny honey

2 tbsp tomato purée/paste

½ tbsp cornflour/cornstarch

200 ml/¾ cup chicken stock

1 tbsp tomato ketchup

1 tsp sherry vinegar

## GAMBAS PIL PIL

125 ml/½ cup olive oil

5 garlic cloves, thickly sliced

½ tsp sweet paprika

3 dried whole chillies/chiles

12 large tiger prawns/jumbo shrimp, head on, shelled and deveined (see page 48)

3 tbsp dry sherry

1 lemon, cut into wedges

a few sprigs of fresh flat-leaf parsley, chopped

salt and freshly ground black pepper

## PADRON PEPPERS

100 g/3½ oz. padrón (small green) peppers

1 tbsp olive oil

1 tsp sea salt flakes

## SANGRIA

1 bottle Spanish red wine

30 g/2½ tbsp sugar

250 ml/1 cup orange juice

100 ml/7 tbsp Spanish brandy

1 orange, sliced

150 g/heaped 1 cup fresh blackberries

1 apple, cored and sliced

400 ml/1¾ cups sparkling water

a handful of ice cubes

## PATATAS BRAVAS

Heat the vegetable oil in a heavy-based pan and once hot, carefully add the potatoes. After 5 minutes add the onion. Deep fry for about 15 minutes until the potatoes are golden and cooked through. If they don't look crispy after 15 minutes, turn the heat up a little. Use a slotted spoon to remove the potatoes and onion and place on paper towels. Season with salt and pepper, then place in a tapas dish.

Add the olive oil, garlic cloves and thyme to a small pan and heat until the garlic sizzles for a couple of minutes, then remove from the heat. Leave to cool for a minute, then whisk in the smoked and sweet paprika, cayenne, honey, tomato purée/paste and cornflour/cornstarch. Once smooth, pour in half the chicken stock, return the pan to the heat and whisk continuously as it thickens, adding more stock as you go. Once bubbling and the consistency of single/light cream, remove from the heat, stir in the tomato ketchup and sherry vinegar and season generously with salt and pepper. Pour over the fried potatoes and onions just before serving and place onto the board.

## PADRON PEPPERS

Fry the peppers in the olive oil over high heat for a few minutes until slightly charred and season generously with sea salt flakes.

**PRESENTATION**
*a large rectangular piece of slate, some small plates and shallow heatproof dishes, such as Spanish terracotta tapas dishes*

*a large jug/pitcher for the sangria plus glass tumblers*

**SERVES 4-6**

## GAMBAS PIL PIL

Heat the olive oil in small pan over a medium heat and cook the garlic slices for a minute, taking care not to let them burn, then add the paprika, chillies/chiles and the prawns/shrimp in a single layer. Fry the prawns/shrimp for a minute on each side, gently pushing down on their heads to release their flavour into the dish. Pour in the sherry and cook for another few minutes to burn off the alcohol, then remove from the heat. Season with salt and a few turns of black pepper, decant into a small dish and garnish with chopped parsley and a few squeezes of lemon juice.

## SANGRIA

Mix the wine and sugar together in a large jug/pitcher until dissolved then add the remaining ingredients and serve (save a few orange wedges to garnish your glasses). If you're feeling adventurous, swap sparkling water for Cava and add another tablespoon of sugar.

## HOW TO ASSEMBLE

Griddle the sliced baguette to give it some colour, then fan out on your board. Place the gambas pil pil and patatas bravas in their tapas plates on the board. Tear a square of baking paper, place on the board and pile the padrón peppers directly onto it. Finally, arrange the olives in a group directly onto the board, along with the breadsticks, chorizo ring and slices and a few glasses of sangria (with the jug/pitcher on the side).

# BUILD-YOUR-OWN
# SUSHI BOWL

I love sushi and sashimi and this board is inspired by both Japanese and Korean flavours. You can, of course, take a shortcut and buy everything in or opt to carve and slice your own fish. It is recommended to freeze fresh fish for a week beforehand to ensure it is suitable to eat raw. Serve your board with chopsticks, green tea and a calm zen-like serenity that is rarely found in our house. (Pictured on pages 112-113.)

100 g/3½ oz. kimchi (from a jar)

3 tbsp soy sauce

2 tsp wasabi paste

20 g/¾ oz. nori sheets (about 7)

1 avocado, halved, stoned/pitted, peeled and sliced on the diagonal

2 carrots, peeled and cut into matchsticks

1 cucumber, halved lengthways, seeds removed, thinly sliced

10 g/2 tsp bonito flakes

50 g/2 oz. salmon roe (or lumpfish roe)

50 g/2 oz. crispy onions

50 g/2 oz. pickled ginger

### SASHIMI

1 mackerel fillet

100 g/½ cup coarse sea salt

250 ml/1 cup rice vinegar

125 g/4½ oz. sashimi-grade salmon

125 g/4½ oz. sashimi-grade tuna

### SUSHI RICE

215 g/heaping 1 cup sushi rice

100 ml/7 tbsp rice vinegar

1 tsp salt

1 tbsp caster/superfine sugar

1 tbsp mixed black and white sesame seeds

### SRIRACHA DIPPING SAUCE

4 tbsp mayonnaise

2 tbsp sriracha sauce

1 tsp freshly squeezed lemon juice

a pinch of salt

### GOCHUJANG DIPPING SAUCE

4 tbsp gochujang paste

½ tbsp sesame oil

1 tbsp runny honey

1 tbsp vinegar

### PRESENTATION
*a large rectangular piece of slate*

### SERVES 4-6

### SASHIMI

Cover the mackerel fillet generously in salt and leave for 45 minutes. Rinse thoroughly to remove the salt, pat dry, then place into a snug bowl with enough rice vinegar to completely submerge and leave for a further 45 minutes. Rinse again and pat dry, then carefully peel off the skin, working from head to tail to reveal the shimmering flesh underneath. Carefully slice widthways.

Using a very sharp knife carefully slice both the salmon and the tuna fillets across the grain into 5-mm/¼-in. slices.

### SUSHI RICE

Rinse the rice a few times in cold running water, then leave in a bowl of cold water to soak for 20 minutes before rinsing one last time. Add the rice and 300 ml/1¼ cups cold water to a saucepan (the water should cover the rice by 2 cm/¾ in.) and bring to a boil. As soon as it bubbles, cover and immediately reduce the heat to very low and cook for 20 minutes. Once cooked, remove the pan from the heat, drain and leave to cool for 10 minutes then tip the rice into a dish, spreading it out to cool further.

While the rice is cooking, mix the rice vinegar with the salt and sugar until dissolved. Sprinkle over the cooked rice and mix together. Keep at room temperature until ready to serve.

### DIPPING SAUCES AND CONDIMENTS

Mix all the ingredients together for each sauce, taste and adjust to suit your preference. Decant into small dipping bowls and set aside until ready to serve.

Place the kimchi and soy sauce into separate dipping bowls and squeeze a little wasabi into the centre of the bowl with the soy sauce.

### HOW TO ASSEMBLE

Lay the sushi rice over two-thirds of the board. Gently flatten the top of the rice and sprinkle over the sesame seeds. Place the mackerel, salmon and tuna sashimi in a line each on top of the rice, with a space between each row but keeping each type of fish grouped together. Now add the dipping sauces and kimchi in their bowls around the board. Slice the nori sheets into 2.5-cm/1-in. strips widthways, roll into little tubes and place in clusters upright around the board. Add the vegetables in neat lines between the rows of fish. Finally, finish the board by nestling pockets of bonito flakes, salmon or lumpfish roe, crispy onions and pickled ginger into any gaps, along with a swirl of wasabi paste.

# 'FRUITS DE MER' PLATTER

I remember the first time I had *fruits de mer* – sitting on a beach in the south of France, feet in the sand, sun on my chest, chilled glass of white wine in my hand and then this beautiful platter of chilled seafood arrived. Heaven! So let's recreate that feeling at home. (Pictured on pages 116–117.)

1 precooked lobster
(approx. 600–800 g/
1 lb. 5 oz.–1 lb. 12 oz.)

800 g/1 lb. 12 oz. precooked
mussels

800 g/1 lb. 12 oz. precooked
crevettes or jumbo prawns/
shrimp

8 precooked langoustines

6 oysters

1 dressed crab

12 whelks in shells

90 g/3 oz. samphire

1 lemon, cut into wedges

Tabasco sauce or Spicy
Tomato Dipping sauce
(see recipe opposite)

sliced baguette, to serve

### AÏOLI

125 ml/⅔ cup mayonnaise

1 garlic clove

1 tsp Dijon mustard

1 tsp freshly squeezed lemon
juice

### PRESENTATION
*a large circular metal
tray with shallow sides,
filled with crushed ice*

### SERVES 4–6

Mix all the aïoli ingredients together, decant into a small dipping bowl, cover and set aside. Make the spicy tomato dipping sauce (see opposite) if using, cover and set aside.

Prepare the lobster by cutting it in half lengthways using a sharp knife, starting at the head, then lowering the knife to cut through the rest of the body. Use the back of the knife to gently crack the claws.

### HOW TO ASSEMBLE
Arrange both halves of the lobster together so it looks whole and nestle it into the ice on one side of the tray. Add the remaining ingredients in clusters rather than mixed and finally fill the gaps between the clusters of seafood with the samphire, dot the lemon wedges around the fish, squeeze in the bowl of aïoli and serve.

Enjoy with a bottle of chilled Chablis and slices of baguette.

# SPICY TOMATO DIPPING SAUCE

A tomato-based cocktail sauce always works well with seafood. Here my recipe is slightly unusual, in that it includes tequila and fresh tomatoes rather than ketchup for a deliciously fresh and tangy accompaniment.

3 small ripe tomatoes
½ garlic clove
½ tbsp cider vinegar
1 tbsp olive oil
1 tbsp tequila blanco
½ tsp Tabasco sauce
1 tsp tomato purée/paste
a generous pinch of salt

**MAKES 200 ML/¾ CUP**

Cut the tomatoes into quarters. Place all the ingredients in a food processor and pulse until smooth. Pass the sauce through a fine sieve/strainer into a small bowl. Taste and add more vinegar or salt if preferred. Pour into a small dish and serve as a dipping sauce alongside the seafood.

# INDIAN-STYLE THALI TRAY

While my wife and I were travelling around India we were introduced to thali – a way of enjoying a selection of delicious dishes all at once. My tray is inspired by memories of what we ate back then. You can, of course, make your own curries (and I've included a couple of recipes for you) but for convenience, good-quality pre-made dishes from your local restaurant will make for a quick yet stunning sharer. I've included my favourite dishes here, but go with whatever you enjoy; in general, I always try to include a meat dish, a vegetable dish, lentil daal, rice, bread and an assortment of pickles. This looks great served on banana leaves which you can easily source online, but this is optional. (Pictured on pages 120–121.)

200 g/1¼ cups basmati rice

400 g/14 oz. precooked beef jalfrezi curry

400 g/14 oz. precooked butter chicken curry

400 g/14 oz. precooked lamb balti curry

200 g/7 oz. precooked sag aloo

3 onion bhajis

3 chapatis or naan breads

100 g/⅓ cup mango chutney

100 g/⅓ cup lime pickle

200 g/¾ cup raita (see recipe on page 52)

a few sprigs of fresh coriander/cilantro

1 lime, cut into wedges

fresh chillies/chiles, to garnish

salt and freshly ground black pepper

**RED LENTIL DAAL**

2 tbsp olive oil

1 onion, diced

2 garlic cloves, crushed

2.5-cm/1-in. piece of fresh ginger, grated

1 tsp ground turmeric

1½ tsp each ground cumin, cumin seeds, garam masala and fennel seeds

1 tbsp tomato purée/paste

200 g/heaping 1 cup red split lentils, rinsed

700 ml/3 cups vegetable stock

400-g/14-oz. can chopped tomatoes

1 tsp nigella seeds

**FRIED FISH MASALA**

1 whole seabass or similar (500–750 g/1 lb. 2 oz.–1 lb. 10 oz.), gutted and cleaned

100 g/3½ oz. tandoori curry paste (must be paste, not curry sauce)

250 ml/1 cup vegetable oil, for frying

**PRESENTATION**
*a large rectangular metal or wooden tray lined with banana leaves*

**SERVES 4–6**

## BASMATI RICE

Add the rice, 500 ml/2 cups water and a pinch of salt to a saucepan and bring to a boil. Cover, reduce the heat to low and cook for 12 minutes. Remove from the heat, cover and set aside until ready to serve.

## RED LENTIL DAAL

Heat the olive oil in a pan, add the diced onion and fry for a few minutes, then add the garlic and ginger and cook for 30 seconds. Add in all the spices, tomato purée/paste and the lentils and stir everything together. Pour in the stock and chopped tomatoes, season, bring to a boil, then reduce the heat to a simmer, cover and cook for 15 minutes.

After 15 minutes, remove the lid, stir the pan to ensure the lentils are not sticking to the bottom and cook, uncovered, for another 5 minutes to thicken, then remove from the heat. Garnish with the nigella seeds.

**FRIED FISH MASALA**

Score each side of the fish, placing the cuts 2.5 cm/1 in. apart. Massage the curry paste all over the fish, including inside the cavity (you can do this up to 1 hour in advance). Heat the vegetable oil in a shallow wok or large pan over a medium heat, then carefully place the fish into the hot oil. Fry the fish for about 5 minutes on each side. Depending on the thickness of your fish this may vary by a couple of minutes. Spoon some of the hot oil inside the cavity while the fish is cooking. Once done, remove the fish from the oil, season with salt and place on paper towels until ready to serve with a few lime wedges.

**HOW TO ASSEMBLE**

Reheat all the precooked curry dishes, onion bhajis, and chapatis or naan according to the package instructions or keep warm if sourced from a take-out restaurant. When you are ready to assemble your board, decant the curries into small warmed bowls, and place the mango chutney, lime pickle and raita into small dipping bowls.

If using, lay banana leaves over your board and start with the rice, tipping it directly onto a banana leaf. You can just use half the rice if it takes up too much room on the board, serving the rest in a bowl on the side. Pile stacks of the chapatis or naan on the board, then place the masala fried fish, kept whole, and placed proudly in the middle of the board. Follow this with the various bowls of curries, dipping sauces and raita and the onion bhajis. Fill any remaining space with sprigs of coriander/cilantro, lime wedges and fresh chillies/chiles.

# SCANDI SMÖRGÅSBORD

Time to get your hygge on! The smörgåsbord is possibly the original sharing platter, and mine boasts Scandi-inspired flavours to build on top of rye bread. In this instance the gravadlax is the star of the show, taking centre stage. I've given simple recipes for some of the dishes, but feel free to buy everything ready-made for convenience if you wish; this is, after all, about sharing time as well as food with your loved ones. Equally, if you don't want to make devilled eggs, simply use hard-boiled eggs with a little mayo dolloped on top.

500 g/1 lb. 2 oz. baby new potatoes

a loaf of rye bread, sliced

1 ripe avocado, halved, stoned/pitted, peeled and sliced on the diagonal

400 g/14 oz. cream cheese, mixed with 2 tbsp creamed horseradish

4 rollmops, sliced in half, skewered

8 radishes, leaves on

1 chicory, leaves separated, to garnish

a few snipped chives, to garnish

sea salt

### GRAVADLAX

2 tbsp juniper berries

1 tbsp coriander seeds

250 g/1 cup white granulated sugar

500 g/2 cups coarse sea salt

1 raw beetroot/beet, grated

4 tbsp gin (not flavoured)

½ side of salmon (about 500 g/1 lb. 2 oz.), deboned, skin on

a handful of fresh dill, to garnish

### GREEN PICKLE

125 ml/½ cup white wine vinegar

1 tbsp caster/superfine sugar

½ tsp salt

1 tbsp mustard seeds

½ cucumber, sliced into thin discs, peel on

a few sprigs of fresh dill, torn

### RED PICKLE

125 ml/½ cup red wine vinegar

1 tbsp caster/superfine sugar

½ tsp salt

1 tbsp coriander seeds

a few turns of cracked black pepper

1 small red onion, thinly sliced

1 large carrot, peeled, diagonally sliced

1 precooked beetroot/beet, cut into rough chunks

2 long red chillies/chiles, whole, pierced once

### GARLIC-DILL DRESSING

1 garlic clove, crushed

4 tbsp olive oil

2 tbsp freshly squeezed lemon juice

a few sprigs of fresh dill, finely chopped

a pinch of salt

### DEVILLED EGGS

5 eggs

2 tbsp mayonnaise

1 tsp Dijon mustard

a pinch of cayenne pepper

50 g/2 oz. lumpfish caviar (or swap for salmon caviar)

### PRESENTATION

*a large oval ceramic or glass platter with shallow sides and a selection of small serving dishes*

### SERVES 6-8

## GRAVADLAX

You will need a large roasting pan with high sides and big enough for the salmon side to lie flat.

To make the curing mixture, grind the juniper berries and coriander seeds together in a pestle and mortar, then combine the spices with the sugar and salt.

Sprinkle about a third of the curing mixture over the bottom of the roasting pan and mix the beetroot into the cure. Drizzle the gin into the salmon flesh, massaging it in, bit by bit, then lay the salmon flesh down into the beetroot/beet cure.

Pour the rest of the curing mixture over the fish, trying to cover the top and sides completely and pat it down. Place a sheet of clingfilm/plastic wrap over the fish, tucking it in around the edges as much as possible, then cover the fish again with another sheet of clingfilm/plastic wrap.

Place a small chopping board or baking sheet on top of the fish, ensuring it fits inside the roasting pan holding the fish. Weight down the board or sheet with a few cans – you need it to be fairly heavy – then pop the whole thing in the fridge.

Leave in the fridge for 2 days (or a maximum of 3). Once a day pour away the juices that gather in the base of the pan. There's no need to remove all the clingfilm/plastic wrap – just open a gap in one corner to pour the liquid away whilst holding the fish in place.

After 2–3 days, remove the fish from the roasting pan, wiping away as much of the curing mixture from the fish as possible. The fish should be nicely firm by now. Rinse the fish under cold water to remove all traces of the cure.

Pat dry with paper towels and cover the flesh side of the salmon with finely chopped dill, patting it down to help it stick. Carve thin slices of the salmon starting at the tail end, carving at an angle towards the tail.

Store any unused fish in the fridge wrapped in baking parchment.

## PICKLES

For both the red and green pickles, mix together the vinegar, sugar and salt until everything is dissolved. Meanwhile, fill your Kilner/Mason-style jars (or other air-tight glass) with the remaining ingredients and pour over the pickling juice, ensuring everything is submerged. Store in the fridge until ready to use.

## POTATOES WITH GARLIC-DILL DRESSING

Boil the potatoes for 12 minutes or until fork tender but not mushy. Drain, season with sea salt and leave to steam dry. Mix the dressing ingredients together, then toss the potatoes into the dressing, cover and set aside.

## DEVILLED EGGS

Place the eggs into a small saucepan, cover with cold water and bring to a boil for 8 minutes. Rinse, peel and slice in half from top to bottom. Carefully scoop out the yolks into a bowl with the mayonnaise, mustard and cayenne pepper and whisk together until fully combined. Spoon the mixture back into the white of the eggs (or pipe it in, if you're feeling fancy) and garnish with a little caviar and chopped chives.

## HOW TO ASSEMBLE

Make a few open rye sandwiches with different toppings (serving any remaining bread on the side), such as:

    Cream cheese, gravadlax, red pickle, chives
    Cream cheese, avocado, green pickle
    Devilled eggs
    Crushed potato with garlic-dill dressing

Lay the gravadlax on the board first, then surround with a few of the open sandwiches and clusters of devilled eggs. Fill small dishes with the red and green pickles and the cream cheese (garnished with a few snipped chives) and place next to the board. Put the dressed potatoes on the board in two clusters, add the avocado halves and rollmops. Fill any gaps with radishes or chicory leaves, dressed with any leftover garlic-dill dressing.

# CHINESE DIM SUM FEAST

Dim sum is a selection of bite-sized Cantonese delicacies traditionally served for a long lazy brunch, but these really are good at any time of day! I once spent a whole afternoon in Beijing making dozens of pork dumplings, but I won't subject you to the same task. Buy in as much as you can, make a few dipping sauces, brew a pot of jasmine green tea and enjoy the rest of the time eating with friends and family. Choose whatever dim sum you enjoy and try to get a variety of steamed, baked and fried for lots of different textures; most can be sourced online or from the frozen section of a large supermarket. (Pictured on pages 128–129.)

6 pork siu mai (steamed pork dumplings)

6 har gow (steamed prawn/shrimp dumplings)

6 char siu bao (steamed BBQ pork buns)

8 mini spring rolls (fried or baked)

6 pot-sticker dumplings

2 slices sesame prawn/shrimp toast, cut into triangles

200 g/7 oz. cheong fun (rice noodle rolls)

3 lo mai gai (sticky rice wrapped in lotus leaf)

8 Chinese-style BBQ spare ribs

lotus root, to garnish

soy sauce, to serve

### GINGER VINEGAR

3 tbsp black rice vinegar

1 tbsp light soy sauce

1 tsp caster/superfine sugar

2.5-cm/1-in. piece of fresh ginger, cut into matchsticks

### CHILLI OIL

50 g/2 oz. chilli/hot red pepper flakes, crushed

½ tsp salt

½ tsp caster/superfine sugar

250 ml/1 cup vegetable oil

1 tbsp Szechuan peppercorns

1 star anise

1 garlic clove

5-cm/2-in. cinnamon stick

### CHOI SUM

200 g/7 oz. choi sum

1 tbsp sesame oil

1 tbsp olive oil

½ chicken stock cube

fresh red chilli/chile, to garnish (optional)

### PRESENTATION

*a large wooden board, bamboo placemats, mini bamboo steamers, banana leaf or baking paper*

### SERVES 4–6

### CHILLI OIL

Mix the chilli/hot red pepper flakes, salt and sugar together in a heatproof bowl or small saucepan. Place over a sieve/strainer above. Add the oil, Szechuan peppercorns, star anise, garlic clove and cinnamon stick to a saucepan and heat until the garlic turns golden, then remove from the heat, leave for a minute, and pour the hot oil through the sieve/strainer into the bowl of chilli/hot red pepper flakes, be careful, it will sizzle! Mix together and, once cool, pour into a sterilized jar and store.

### GINGER VINEGAR

Mix all the ingredients together in a bowl with a tablespoon of water and leave to infuse before serving.

### CHOI SUM

Halve the choi sum where the stalk meets the leaves. Heat the sesame oil and olive oil in a frying pan or skillet and, when hot, add the stalks and leaves and fry for 2 minutes. Crumble in the stock cube, add 2 tablespoons of water and continue cooking for another minute. Remove from the heat and serve. If you wish, garnish with a few slithers of fresh red chilli/chile.

### HOW TO ASSEMBLE

Cook all the dim sum according to the package instructions, plus the spare ribs and choi sum and keep warm. Fill a few dipping bowls with the chilli/chili oil, ginger vinegar, soy sauce and/or any other sauces you like.

Lay the bamboo placemats over your board with a few mini bamboo steamers filled with dim sum. Place some of the bigger delicacies (rice wrapped in lotus leaves, ribs, spring rolls) directly onto a cut piece of banana leaf or baking parchment onto the board.

Place the rolled noodles and the choi sum (or any other greens) snugly together on a plate, drizzle a little chilli/chili oil over the rolled noodles and place both plates on the board. Finish by squeezing in the bowls of dipping sauces around the board.

Serve with jasmine green tea, small side plates and chopsticks.

# PLOUGHMAN'S PLATTER

I like to think of the origins of the ploughman's lunch – a hearty meal fit for satisfying the hunger after a long morning toiling the fields. However, the reality is now an awesome grazing board, usually found in a British pub accompanied by a pint of ale. As the ingredients are simple fare, buy the best quality you can afford, from the cheese and ham to the butter.

1 Cumberland ring sausage, cooked

200 g/7 oz. mature Cheddar

200 g/7 oz. Stilton

1 large pork pie (or 2 smaller ones)

100 g/3½ oz. rustic pâté

200 g/7 oz. smoked ham, thickly sliced

a small rustic loaf, e.g. multi-seed sourdough loaf

1 pear, sliced

2 small tart eating apples

1 buffalo (steak) tomato, sliced

3 tbsp English mustard

100 g/3½ oz. piccalilli

100 g/3½ oz. Branston pickle

3 tbsp caramelized onion chutney

3 soft-boiled eggs, peeled and halved

a handful of radishes

50 g/2 oz. cornichons

50 g/2 oz. pickled onions

a few leafy celery stalks/ribs

salt and freshly ground black pepper

butter, to serve

## PRESENTATION
*a large rustic wooden board and some small dishes*

SERVES 4–6

## HOW TO ASSEMBLE

The cumberland sausage ring should be the largest ingredient so add that to the board first, just off-centre. Next arrange the cheeses, pork pie (either left whole or sliced), pâté and sliced ham on the broad. Next introduce the apples, pears, sliced tomato and celery in different spots on the board and fan out the slices.

Add a dish of butter to the board. Spoon the chutney, pickle, piccalilli and mustard into small dishes and place next to the cheeses, with the English mustard next to the ham. (If any of the pickles have a thicker consistency, they can be spooned in dollops directly onto the board.) Add slices of bread around the outside edge of the board.

Finally, add the halved soft-boiled eggs (or hard-boiled if you prefer) in three groups of two, cut side up with a pinch of salt on the top of each one. Lastly, fill the gaps with the the smaller foods, such as radishes, cornichons, pickled onions and leafy celery stalks/ribs.

CHAPTER

5

# Seasonal Celebrations

# VALENTINE'S DAY LOVE LETTERS

What better way to show your love than with a love letter you can eat!
This beautiful board is all about scrawling sweet nothings on edible rice
paper and sticking them to your choice of cookies and shortbread, or even
thin blocks of chocolate. Use a selection of shapes and sizes, but try to
have them as flat as possible. I've also included some edible butterflies.

6 sheets edible rice/
wafer paper

8 biscuits/cookies of
your choice

8 shortbread fingers
and/or fans

100 g/3½ oz. chocolate,
cut ito pieces

3 x colours of edible dust

a selection of cake pens

edible glitter spray

edible/food-safe flowers,
to decorate

candied rhubarb strings
(optional)

**PRESENTATION**
*any board of your choice
can be used, but a pretty
marble slab works well*

*brushes*

*butterfly punch*

*ribbon or string/twine*

**SERVES 2-4**

Cut out some pieces of rice/wafer paper to the same sizes and shapes
as some of your cookies, shortbread and chocolate pieces. Lightly
brush each piece or rice/wafer paper with water and sprinkle with
different coloured edible dust. Carefully write little words of love on
each one using a cake pen. Let dry.

Set aside a couple of biscuits/cookies or shortbreads to build a stack
of letters.

Lightly wet the top edge of the remaining biscuits/cookies, shortbread
and chocolate pieces with water (I wet my finger and run it around
the edge) and carefully place the finished rice paper/wafer note on
top, pressing around the edge to stick it in place. If it smudges, you can
always brush the edges with a little more edible dust. Set aside.

For the butterflies, take some rice paper and use the butterfly punch
to cut out a few edible butterflies. Fold each one in half and open it
out again. You can decorate the butterflies as you like with edible glitter
spray and/or cake pens.

### HOW TO ASSEMBLE
Add the paper-topped biscuits/cookies, shortbread and chocolate to
the board. Dot some of the butterflies around the board and stick some
butterflies to the corner of the love letters (run a wet finger along the
bottom of the butterfly so it sticks).

Create a 'stack' of love letters by placing two biscuits/cookies together
(without rice paper/wafer), place a finished love letter on top and tie
together with ribbon or candied rhubarb strings, as shown. Decorate
the board with some edible, food-safe flowers.

# GIANT EASTER CHOCOLATE SLAB

My giant chocolate slab is a great way to use up a surfeit of Easter celebration chocolate, while creating something delightful and delicious to share over the weekend. I like to use melted chocolate shells as the base of the board, then stick lots of fun bits on top, from bunnies to brownies.

500 g/1 lb. 2 oz. dark/
bittersweet and milk
chocolate Easter eggs
(or use chocolate bars)

1 large chocolate Easter
bunny (or 5 smaller ones)

150 g/5 oz. white chocolate

200 g/7 oz. chocolate
brownie, cut into chunks

3 Cadbury creme eggs,
halved

a handful of different
coloured mini
marshmallows

50 g/generous ⅓ cup
hazelnuts, crushed

**PRESENTATION**
*this can be served on a tray,
but is also just as lovely
served in the sheetpan
you make it it*

*25 x 38-cm/10 x 15-in.
deep-sided baking sheet,
lined with baking parchment*

**SERVES 6-8**

Preheat the oven to 90°C fan/110°C/225°F/Gas ¼.

Break the Easter eggs or bars of chocolate into pieces and arrange on the paper lined-baking sheet.

Use a serrated knife (or carefully break away) one side of the Easter bunny (so it will lay in profile, facing up). Set the bunny aside and add the broken bits of chocolate to the baking sheet.

Place the baking sheet into the preheated oven for 10 minutes.

Meanwhile, break the white chocolate into a heat-proof bowl and place above a saucepan of simmering water (making sure the water isn't touching the bowl). Stir with a wooden spoon until it is mainly melted, but still with a few lumps, then immediately remove the bowl from the saucepan and continue stirring until smooth.

Remove the baking sheet from the oven and gently drizzle the white chocolate over the melted chocolate and swirl the it around using a cocktail stick/toothpick or small knife to make pretty patterns.

**HOW TO ASSEMBLE**

While still slightly soft, gently press the chocolate bunny (facing up) into the melted chocolate along with the creme egg halves (facing yolk side up). Nestle small chunks of the brownie all over the melted chocolate.

Next, scatter the marshmallows into the melted chocolate and finish with a few clusters of crushed hazelnuts here and there.

Leave to cool and set at room temperature, then carefully cut the baking parchment to the size of the chocolate (or peel off the paper if the chocolate is strong enough) and place on a tray to serve.

# MOTHER'S DAY AFTERNOON TEA BOARD

For my wife's birthday one year we created a gorgeous afternoon tea at home. This board was inspired by that day. Perfect for Mother's Day.

6 ready-made scones

250 g/9 oz. strawberry jam/preserve

250 g/9 oz. clotted cream or whipped double/heavy cream

12–16 mini desserts of your choice

8 macarons of your choice

tea and milk, to serve

### SMOKED SALMON FINGER SANDWICHES

4 tbsp cream cheese

1 tbsp creamed horseradish

2 slices wholemeal bread, lightly buttered

90 g/3 oz. smoked salmon

a handful of salad cress

freshly ground black pepper

### CUCUMBER FINGER SANDWICHES

2 slices white bread, heavily buttered

¼ cucumber, peeled and thinly sliced

salt and freshly ground black pepper

### EGG MAYONNAISE FINGER SANDWICHES

1 hard-boiled egg, chopped

1½ tbsp mayonnaise

¼ tsp freshly squeezed lemon juice

a pinch of cayenne pepper

2 slices white bread, buttered

a handful of salad cress

salt

### HAM AND CHEESE FINGER SANDWICHES

1 tsp English mustard

2 slices rye bread, buttered

60 g/2 oz. thick-cut ham

60 g/2 oz. Cheddar cheese, sliced

1 tbsp fine-cut pickle

### SMOKED SALMON FINGER SANDWICHES

Mix the cream cheese and creamed horseradish together, then spread over one slice of the buttered bread. Arrange the smoked salmon on top, then scatter with the cress. Add a grinding of black pepper. Top with the other slice of buttered bread, trim away the crusts and cut into four fingers.

### CUCUMBER FINGER SANDWICHES

Sprinkle salt and pepper over one slice of the buttered bread. Arrange slices of cucumber on the bread. Top with the other slice of buttered bread, trim away the crusts and cut into four fingers.

### EGG MAYONNAISE FINGER SANDWICHES

Mix the egg with the mayonnaise, lemon juice, cayenne and a pinch of salt. Spread over one slice of buttered bread and then scatter with the cress. Top with the other slice of buttered bread, trim the crusts and cut into four fingers.

### HAM AND CHEESE FINGER SANDWICHES

Spread the mustard on one piece of bread and top with the ham, cheese and pickle. Top with the other slice of buttered bread, trim away the crusts and cut into four fingers.

TIP: To get a nice uniform stack of mixed sandwiches, stack them on top of each other and use a sharp serrated knife to trim the crusts and cut into fingers.

## PRESENTATION

*a slate or marble slab looks really stylish, or you could use a silver tray for an elegant look*

*a bone china teapot, teacups and saucers*

**SERVES 4**

## HOW TO ASSEMBLE

You have several components to a traditional afternoon tea; the finger sandwiches, the scones with cream and jam/preserve and the mini sweet desserts and macarons – and not forgetting the all important tea to drink!

Place the finger sandwiches in four uniform stacks around the board.

Pile the scones in one area. Put the jam/preserve and clotted cream in little serving bowls and place them adjacent to the scones.

Group the mini desserts together and arrange them on the board. Use the macarons to fill in any gaps.

Place the teapot, milk jug, sugar bowl and cups and saucers around the board.

# FATHER'S DAY BBQ BOARD

One for the dads, but this board serves at least four as I always have to share it with my wife and kids! The great thing about this Father's Day board is you can put everything in the oven (more or less at the same time), assemble the board and you're good to go!

BBQ Ribs (see recipe on page 146) or use 950-g/ 2-lb. packet of precooked BBQ ribs

4 half corn-on-the-cobs

4–6 sausages

3 Portobello mushrooms

200 g/7 oz. on-the-vine cherry tomato stems

500 g/1 lb. 2 oz. frozen sweet potato oven chips

Onion Rings (see recipe on page 147) or use 12 frozen onion rings

200 g/7 oz. coleslaw

4 tbsp Dijon mustard

4 tbsp mayonnaise

a handful of cornichons or use 2 large gherkins/dill pickles, halved lengthways

a handful of salad leaves

craft beer, to serve (optional)

**PRESENTATION**
*a wooden board lined with baking parchment works or a metal tray is ideal*

**SERVES 4–6**

Preheat the oven to 180°C fan/200°C/400°F/Gas 6.

If you are making your own ribs, prepare these first following the recipe on page 146.

Wrap the corn-on-the-cobs in foil and place in the preheated oven. After 15 minutes, put the sausages in a baking pan and place in the oven and continue cooking both for 15 minutes. Now add the mushrooms and tomatoes to the baking pan with the sausages and continue to cook everything for a further 10 minutes. (The corn will need a total of 40 minutes; the sausages 25 minutes; the mushrooms and tomatoes 10 minutes.)

Cook the ribs (if using precooked), chips and onion rings (if using frozen) according to the package instructions and keep warm. If making your own onion rings, prepare these according to the recipe on page 147.

**HOW TO ASSEMBLE**
When everything is cooked you can build your board.

Start with the ribs, which will take up the most space. Put these in the middle of the board. If you like, you can cut these into four–six smaller racks and pile them up, or serve them with a carving knife. Group the sausages together along with the corn, chips, onion rings, mushrooms and tomatoes.

Decant the coleslaw into a bowl and add to the board. Put the mustard, any leftover BBQ sauce and mayonnaise into small bowls and place on the board. Add the pickled cornichons and fill the final gaps with the salad leaves. Serve with glasses craft beer, if liked.

# BBQ RIBS

These juicy BBQ ribs are oven-baked and fall-off-the bone delicious. You double up on flavour by using a dry spice rub before cooking and then slathering them with a tasty BBQ sauce part-way through cooking. The leftover sauce can be used as a condiment. You can also make up a batch of the sauce to serve with my Game-night Wings 'n' dips Tray (see page 72) or simply enjoy as a dipper for hot chips.

500–750 g/1 lb. 2 oz.–
   1 lb. 10 oz. pork ribs

1 tbsp sea salt flakes

1 tbsp smoked paprika

1 tbsp ground cumin

1 tsp garlic granules

1 tsp cayenne pepper

1 onion, sliced

**BBQ SAUCE**

100 ml/scant ½ cup ketchup

3 tbsp dark soy sauce

2 tbsp runny honey

1 tbsp vinegar

1 tbsp Bourbon

salt

**MAKES 4 SERVINGS**

Preheat the oven to 160°C fan/180°C/350°F/Gas 4.

To prepare the ribs, remove the membrane from the back. To do this, slide the back of a spoon or blunt knife inbetween the meat and the membrane to separate them, then peel off the membrane.

Mix the salt and dried spices together, then rub the dry mixture over the ribs on both sides.

Lay a flat sheet of baking paper on the work surface and scatter over half the sliced onion. Place the ribs on top and then scatter the remaining onion on top of the ribs. Fold the paper over to make a parcel, and finally wrap the whole thing in foil. Place in the preheated oven and cook for 2 hours.

Mix all the BBQ sauce ingredients together with a pinch of salt and set aside.

Once the ribs have been cooking for 2 hours, remove the parcel from the oven (leaving it wrapped for now) and turn the temperature up to 220°C fan/240°C/475°F/Gas 9.

Once the oven reaches temperature, open the parcel to reveal the ribs. Liberally brush the ribs with some of the BBQ sauce (reserving some for serving) and return to the oven (with the parcel still open) for 5–10 minutes, just long enough for the sauce to get sticky and form a glaze.

Drizzle over the reserved sauce and serve.

# ONION RINGS

Home-made deep-fried crispy onion rings are surprisingly simple to make and melt-in-the-mouth delicious. These would make a great addition to the Bespoke Burger Board (see page 54), or you can just knock a batch up to enjoy with a cold beer as an anytime snack. Ring the changes flavour-wise too by replacing the cayenne with Spanish smoked paprika or even a mild curry powder.

1 large egg

125 ml/½ cup whole/full-fat milk

150 g/generous 1 cup plain/all-purpose flour

1 tsp cayenne pepper

2 large white onions, sliced into 5-mm/¼-in. thick rings

vegetable oil, for frying

**MAKES 4 SERVINGS**

In one bowl mix the egg and milk together, then in separate bowl mix the flour and cayenne together. Set aside.

Submerge the onion rings in the milk and egg mixture for a few minutes. When you are ready to cook, heat the oil in a large, heavy-based pan, at least 2.5 cm/1 in. deep until a small piece of onion sizzles but does not burn.

Working in batches, shake off the excess liquid from the rings, drop them into the flour and cayenne mixture to coat and gently place them into the hot oil. Cook for about 5–6 minutes until golden, then remove with a slotted spoon and drain on paper towels.

Season with a pinch of salt and serve.

# SUMMER GARDEN CRUDITÉS

This summertime crudités board is about creating your own edible garden; you can buy in pretty much everything with only the 'olive soil' to make. The idea is to build your garden, so choose whatever type of dips you like – just ensure they are quite thick and not runny. (Pictured on pages 148–149.)

## OLIVE 'SOIL'

500 g/1 lb. 2 oz. pitted black olives (drained weight), rinsed and dried

## VINAIGRETTE

4 tbsp olive oil

2 tbsp white wine vinegar

1 tsp Dijon mustard

a pinch of dried oregano (optional)

salt and freshly ground black pepper

## ON THE SIDE VEGETABLES

3 baby cucumbers, quartered lengthways

1 baby gem lettuce, leaves separated

12 asparagus spears

## DIPS

350 g/12 oz. hummus

350 g/12 oz. guacamole

350 g/12 oz. cream cheese and chive dip

## GARDEN VEGETABLES

12 radishes, leaves on

4 baby beetroot/beets (golden, candy or red), leaves on

6 slim heritage carrots, leaves on

12 on-the-vine piccolo tomatoes

3 chives, cut into 5-cm/2-in. lengths

## PRESENTATION

*a wooden or metal tray and small plant pot-style pots or mini buckets*

## SERVES 4–6

Preheat the oven to 70°C fan/90°C/190°F/lowest gas setting.

For the olive 'soil', bake the olives in the preheated oven for 8 hours or until brittle. Let cool. Pulse in food processor (not blender) until you have a fine crumb. Store in an airtight container.

In a jar or small bowl, whisk together the vinaigrette ingredients. Set aside.

Divide the 'on the side' vegetables into a few small plant pots or mini buckets.

## HOW TO ASSEMBLE

Place the small dipping bowl near one corner of the board, sticking it in place with a teaspoon of hummus. Now spoon out the dips in a thick layer widthways over one third each of the board – going snugly around the dipping bowl – so you end up with three stripes of dips. Scatter the olive 'soil' over the whole board (not the dipping bowl) covering all the dips in one layer to create your 'garden'. At this stage you should have a solid black surface with the dipping bowl in one corner (brush any olive 'soil' from inside the dipping bowl). Save a little olive 'soil' for touching up later.

Give the 'garden' vegetables a quick wash, then trim any long leaves from the top, leaving a couple on each one. (For the radishes, you can trim a thin layer from the bottom so they stand upright and 'plant' them lightly in the garden, if liked.)

Cut the baby beetroot/beets in half and add to the board along with the carrots, tomatoes and chives. Finally, pour the vinaigrette into the bowl.

Touch up any gaps with the reserved olive 'soil'.

Serve the board with the plant pots or mini buckets of the 'on the side' vegetables for dipping.

# SNOW DAY FONDUE

Cosy jumpers, roaring fire, enough melted cheese and wine to sink a battleship – what could be better! My snow day fondue is a fun way to eat with friends; everyone dunking and eating and joining in! If you don't have a fondue set, don't worry, a good cast-iron or copper pot warmed through will keep the fondue warm and silky until you're scraping the bottom for the last smidge to go on your bread!

500 g/1 lb. 2 oz. baby new potatoes

12 asparagus spears

2 tbsp butter

2 pears

1 sourdough loaf, cut into 4-cm/1½-in. cubes

285-g/10-oz. jar cornichons and baby pickled onions, drained

2 figs, halved

1 stick/rib celery, cut into 4-cm/1½-in pieces

## FONDUE

1 small garlic clove, crushed

a pinch of grated nutmeg

400 ml/1¾ cups white wine

300 g/2½ cups grated Gouda or Emmental

300 g/2½ cups grated Gruyère or Comté

100 g/generous ¾ cup Cambozola, Taleggio or Dolcelatte, cut into chunks

2 tbsp brandy

1 tbsp cornflour/cornstarch, plus extra if needed

## PRESENTATION
*a round wooden board means everyone can reach the fondue pot easily*

*skewers or long fondue forks*

**SERVES 6–8**

Boil the potatoes for 12 minutes or until they are fork tender but not mushy, drain, season with sea salt and leave to steam dry.

Fry the asparagus spears in the butter for a few minutes, then let cool.

Quarter the pears, leaving the skin on. Cover with a damp tea/dish towel.

Leave the cubed sourdough open to the air to help it dry out a little.

Pour all the fondue ingredients – except the brandy and cornflour/cornstarch into a large saucepan and gently bring to a simmer, stirring all the time. Season with salt and pepper.

Once the cheese has melted and the wine has started bubbling, turn the heat down.

Make a slurry with the brandy and cornflour/cornstarch and stir into the fondue. Keep it on the heat until the mixture thickens and becomes smooth, then remove from the heat. (If it splits or looks grainy, add another tablespoon cornflour/cornstarch with a little water and stir continulously over the heat to bring it back together.)

## HOW TO ASSEMBLE
Pour the mixture into a warmed fondue, cast-iron or copper pot and place in the middle of the board. Add a little freshly grated nutmeg to the top of the fondue for a nice touch.

Add the cornichons and onions to the board in little ramekins, then fill the board with clusters of potatoes, asparagus, pear slices, sourdough cubes, figs and celery. Serve immediately!

# HALLOWEEN WARMER

This grown-up board is dark and spooky, with cups of spiced pumpkin soup and tasty nibbles. You can use store-bought soup, or make your own using my recipe. You can also make a black hummus by using black chickpeas/garbanzo beans – they are available from most supermarkets or online. (Pictured on pages 154–155.)

6 slices black sourdough

500 g/3⅓ cups black sable grapes

200 g/2 cups pitted black olives

12 cheese-stuffed Peppadew peppers

3 toffee apples, store-bought or homemade

black sesame seeds, to garnish

**PUMPKIN SOUP**

1 tbsp olive oil

1 kg/2 lb. 4 oz. pumpkin or squash flesh, cut into 2.5-cm/1-in. cubes

a few sprigs of thyme

1 small onion, finely chopped

50 g/3½ tbsp butter

1 garlic clove, sliced

a pinch of ground turmeric

a pinch of ground ginger

about 500 ml/2 cups chicken or vegetable stock

salt and white pepper

**HUMMUS**

400-g/14-oz. can chickpeas/garbanzo beans, drained (save the liquid)

1 garlic clove, crushed

1 tbsp freshly squeezed lemon juice, or to taste

1 tbsp olive oil

1 tbsp tahini

½ tsp salt, or to taste

**PRESENTATION**

*a black slate is very effective here with black cups for serving the soup*

**SERVES 4**

### HUMMUS

Add all the ingredients to a food processor and the reserved liquid from the can (aquafaba). Pulse until smooth, then add the aquafaba, a little at a time, until the hummus is thick but pliable. Taste, adding more lemon juice or salt as needed.

### PUMPKIN SOUP

Preheat the oven to 200°C fan/220°C/425°C/Gas 7.

Drizzle the oil over the pumpkin cubes and season with salt and white pepper. Arrange the thyme on a baking sheet and put the pumpkin on top. Roast in the preheated oven for 30 minutes until soft.

Meanwhile, fry the onion in the butter on a low heat for about 6 minutes until soft and slightly caramelized, then add the garlic. After another few minutes, stir in the turmeric, ginger, a pinch of white pepper and half the stock, then remove from the heat. Once the pumpkin is cooked, add it to the pan and bring to a boil, then remove from the heat and blend until smooth, adding more stock until you reach the consistency of double/heavy cream.

Pass through a sieve/strainer to ensure it is silky, and season to taste. Pour into coffee cups.

### HOW TO ASSEMBLE

Add the soup cups to your board and spoon the hummus directly onto the board. Garnish the soup and hummus with a sprinkle of black sesame seeds.

Lay the black sourdough on the board and fill the gaps with the grapes, black olives, Pepperdew peppers and toffee apples.

# THANKSGIVING BOARD

While living in America, Thanksgiving was my favourite time of year; huge feasts of gratitude surrounded by friends and family. Much of this board includes classic recipes, but I've given the sweet potato marshmallow bake an upgrade – you can buy all of this pre-made from supermarkets/grocery stores or use leftovers from Thanksgiving and serve it the next day. (Pictured on pages 158–159.)

1 kg/2 lb. 4 oz. heritage carrots, peeled

1 tbsp butter

1 tbsp runny honey

a pinch of caraway seeds

a pinch of sea salt flakes

600 g/6 cups Brussels sprouts, halved

1 tbsp olive oil

500 g/1 lb. 2 oz. chestnut stuffing balls

6–8 oven-ready potato buns

1 litre/4 cups turkey gravy

1.4–1.8-kg/3–4-lb. smoked turkey crown, cooked and sliced (or leftover turkey)

a jar of cranberry sauce

6–8 leafy clementines

1 red chicory, leaves separated

salt and freshly ground black pepper

### SWEET POTATO MARSHMALLOW BAKE

1 kg/2 lb. 4 oz. sweet potato, peeled and cubed

5 rashers/slices smoked streaky/fatty bacon, chopped

a little oil, for frying

2 tbsp butter

1 tbsp maple syrup

1 tsp ground cinnamon

a pinch of allspice

200 g/5 cups mini marshmallows

### PARMESAN MASHED POTATOES

1 kg/2 lb. 4 oz. white potatoes, such as Maris Piper, peeled and cubed

40 g/½ cup grated Parmesan cheese, plus extra to garnish

50 g/3½ tbsp butter

3 tbsp milk

12 chives, chopped

### PRESENTATION
*a large wooden board works well, or choose a purple one, as here, to offset the autumnal colours*

*1.5-litre/6-cup round skillet or baking dish*

### SERVES 6–8

Preheat the oven to 200°C fan/220°C/425°C/Gas 7.

If the carrots have leaves on, wrap them in a little foil. Halve any carrots that are very thick. Simmer the carrots in salted boiling water for about 8 minutes, then drain and leave to steam dry. Once dry, arrange the carrots on a baking sheet, dot with butter, cover with foil and bake in the preheated oven for 30 minutes until tender. Remove the foil, turn the carrots over in the butter, drizzle the honey over and sprinkle on the caraway seeds. Return to the oven for 5 minutes. Finish with a pinch of sea salt flakes.

While the carrots are cooking, add the halved Brussels sprouts to a roasting pan, drizzle with the olive oil, season and roast in the preheated oven for 20 minutes, or until slightly charred.

Cook the stuffing balls and potato buns according to the package instructions. Warm the gravy through.

### SWEET POTATO MARSHMALLOW BAKE
Preheat the oven to 200°C fan/220°C/425°C/Gas 7.

Cook the sweet potato in salted boiling water until tender. Meanwhile, fry the bacon in a little oil until crisp, then drain on paper towels. Once cooked, drain the sweet potatoes and leave to steam dry, then mash thoroughly. While still warm, fold in the butter, maple syrup, cinnamon and allspice, and season to taste.

Spoon into the skillet or baking dish and smooth the top with the back of a spoon.

Scatter the bacon bits evenly over the top and finish with a single layer of marshmallows. Bake in a preheated oven for 20 minutes or until the marshmallows are golden. (If making in advance, reheat the sweet potato mash in the oven without the toppings, then, once warmed through, add the bacon and marshmallows and place under a grill/broiler to brown the marshmallows.)

## PARMESAN MASHED POTATOES

Cook the white potatoes in salted boiling water until tender. Drain and leave to steam dry completely before mashing thoroughly. While still warm, fold in the grated Parmesan, butter and milk, and season to taste with a generous pinch of salt and pepper.

## HOW TO ASSEMBLE

Place the turkey in the middle of a large wooden board. Add the sweet potato bake, still in its skillet. Spoon on the mashed potatoes in two piles and top with a little extra Parmesan and the chopped chives. Add the cranberry sauce in a small bowl. Pour the warm gravy into a jug/pitcher and add to the board. Dot the buns in groups on the board, and add the carrots and Brussels sprouts directly on the board.

Fill the gaps with clementines (cut some in half) and chicory leaves for colour.

# CHRISTMAS TREATS TRAY

This is my Christmas treats tray, seasonal flavours (and aromas) brought together in some fun recipes, ready to enjoy with glasses of mulled wine in front of a roaring fire. From cute and easy to make Christmas Pudding Baubles to Mince-pie Pinwheels. (Pictured on pages 162–163.)

250 ml/1 cup brandy cream

6 clementines with leaves

6 store-bought decorate-your-own gingerbread men with icing pens

### CHRISTMAS PUDDING BAUBLES

350 g/12 oz. leftover Christmas pudding or rich fruit cake

100 g/3½ oz. dark/bittersweet chocolate (70 per cent cocoa), broken

300 g/10½ oz. white chocolate, broken

red and gold oil-based food colouring

red, gold and silver edible dust (optional)

### WALNUT AND CINNAMON MINCE-PIE PINWHEELS

plain/all-purpose flour, for dusting

320 g/11 oz. puff pastry dough

2 tbsp melted butter

1 tbsp ground cinnamon

grated zest of 1 clementine

50 g/generous ⅓ cup walnuts, chopped

1 tbsp brandy

400 g/1¾ cups mincemeat/mince pie filling

1 egg, beaten

2 tbsp icing/confectioner's sugar

### PRESENTATION
*a round metal tray works well with the sparkly Christmas pudding baubles*

*a few cocktail sticks/toothpicks or skewers*

**SERVES 4-6**

### CHRISTMAS PUDDING BAUBLES

Mash the leftover Christmas pudding in a bowl. Melt the dark/bittersweet chocolate in the microwave in 20-second bursts, stirring in between, then pour into the mashed Christmas pudding and mix thoroughly. Working quickly, roll out ping pong ball-sized balls and place in the fridge for 20 minutes.

Meanwhile, melt the white chocolate in the microwave in 20-second bursts, stirring in between, then divide into three warm bowls. Add red colouring to one, gold to another and leave one plain.

Insert a cocktail stick/toothpick into the pudding balls and dip each one into one of the bowls of coloured melted chocolate, then place on a wire rack to set. You should have three sets of different coloured balls. Once almost dry, you can dust with the matching edible dust to give them a shimmer, if you like – use silver on the white ones. Store in an airtight container until ready to use.

## WALNUT AND CINNAMON MINCE-PIE PINWHEELS

Preheat the oven to 200°C fan/220°C/425°C/Gas 7.

On a lightly dusted work surface roll out the pastry into a rectangular shape about 3 mm/⅛ in. thick. Brush the surface with the melted butter, then sprinkle over the ground cinnamon, half the clementine zest and the chopped walnuts. Mix the brandy with the mincemeat/mince pie filling until fully incorporated, then spoon over the pastry in an even layer.

With the longest side nearest to you, roll the pastry into a log, brushing the final edge of the pastry with the beaten egg to stick it together. Place in the fridge for 10 minutes (this makes it easier to cut).

Use a sharp knife to cut the log into 1.5-cm/½-inch slices and place onto the lined baking sheet. Brush the remaining beaten egg over the top.

Bake in the preheated oven for about 15 minutes until the pastry is puffed and golden. Remove from the oven and leave to cool.

## HOW TO ASSEMBLE

Put the brandy cream in a bowl, sprinkle with a little clementine zest and place on the tray. Arrange the decorated gingerbread men, mince pie pinwheels and Christmas pudding baubles (you can mount these on sticks in the style of cake pops, if liked). If you are serving mulled wine, you can add heatproof cups of this to the tray too and carry it to the fireside all together.

# BOXING DAY BUFFET BOARD

Leftovers from Christmas Day are an inevitable part of Boxing Day so why not use them to create a delicious board? As this uses leftovers, don't worry if you have a bit more or less than what's listed, the point is to use up what you have lurking in the kitchen. (Pictured on pages 166–167.)

a handful of spinach leaves

any leftover ham or other cold cuts, sliced

a few sticks/ribs of celery with leaves

salt and freshly ground black pepper

### CORONATION TURKEY

30 g/¼ cup dried apricots, finely chopped

a pinch of saffron or ground turmeric

2 tbsp curry powder

100 g/scant ½ cup mayonnaise

100 g/scant ½ cup natural/plain Greek yogurt

½ tbsp Worcestershire sauce

1 tsp freshly squeezed lemon juice, or to taste

about 500 g/1 lb. 2 oz. leftover turkey, shredded

1 kg/2 lb. 4 oz. waxy new potatoes, boiled and halved (optional)

2 tbsp toasted flaked/slivered almonds

### BUBBLE AND SQUEAK

about 1 kg/2 lb. 4 oz. leftover vegetables (potatoes, carrots, parsnips, Brussels sprouts, etc.)

1 small egg, beaten

1 tbsp wholegrain mustard

1 tsp Worcestershire sauce

a pinch of chilli flakes/hot red pepper flakes

1 tbsp olive oil

1 tbsp butter

4–6 fried eggs, to serve

### PIGS IN BLANKETS

12 pre-made pigs in blankets

100 g/⅓ cup cranberry sauce

1 tbsp hot water

a pinch of thyme leaves

### CRANBERRY AND TOMATO BRUSCHETTA

1 small baguette, sliced 1 cm/½ in. thick

2 tbsp olive oil

4 tsp cider vinegar

2 ripe on-the-vine tomatoes, chopped

a small bunch of parsley, chopped

80 g/generous ½ cup dried cranberries, coarsely chopped

½ red onion, finely chopped

### PRESENTATION
*you will need a large wooden board for this*

### SERVES 4–6

## CORONATION TURKEY

Put the dried apricots in a bowl and add just enough boiling water to cover. Add the saffron (or turmeric) and let steep until ready to use.

Lightly toast the curry powder in a dry frying pan or skillet for a minute (careful not to burn) then tip into a mixing bowl with the mayonnaise, yogurt, Worcestershire sauce, lemon juice and a pinch of salt and pepper. Pour in the apricots and their soaking liquid and mix thoroughly to combine.

Put the shredded leftover turkey in a bowl and add the coronation sauce, a little at a time, until it is well coated (you may have some Coronation sauce left over depending on how much turkey you have, if so, use this to dress the boiled new potatoes, if using). If it's a little thick you can add a splash of water. Taste, adding salt or more lemon juice to taste.

## BUBBLE AND SQUEAK

Chop all the leftover vegetables and place in a bowl. Bash with a potato masher until you have a coarse paste, then fold in the egg, wholegrain mustard, Worcestershire sauce, chilli flakes/hot red pepper flakes and season with salt and pepper. Mix thoroughly and shape into burger-sized patties about 2 cm/¾ in. thick. (If your veg is quite moist, you can omit the egg.)

Heat the oil and butter in a heavy-based frying pan or skillet and lay each patty into the hot pan – don't move them! Cook for 4 minutes on medium-high heat, or until they form a deep golden crust, then carefully flip and cook for 4 minutes more. Remove from the pan. Serve with the fried eggs.

### PIGS IN BLANKETS

Cook the pigs in blankets according to the package instructions. Meanwhile, slightly water down the cranberry sauce with the hot water. About 5 minutes before the end of their cooking time, liberally brush the pigs in blankets with the cranberry sauce and return to the oven. Once done, give them a final brush with the cranberry sauce and garnish with a pinch of thyme leaves.

### CRANBERRY AND TOMATO BRUSCHETTA

Preheat the oven to 200°C fan/220°C/425°C/Gas 7.

Brush the baguette slices in a little olive oil and toast in the preheated oven for 5 minutes, turning over halfway through. Let cool.

Mix the remaining ingredients together in a bowl and season to taste.

When ready to serve, use a fork to spoon the cranberry and tomato topping generously onto the sliced baguette.

### HOW TO ASSEMBLE

Place a handful of spinach leaves directly onto the board and spoon out the coronation turkey (and dressed potatoes) directly onto the spinach leaves (these act as a plate on your board). Sprinkle the flaked/sliced almonds on top.

Add the bubble and squeak patties to the board, topping some of them with fried eggs. Add the cranberry and tomato bruschetta to the board along with a cluster of the glazed pigs in blankets. Finally, finish with any leftover cold cuts and fill the gaps with a few small celery sticks dotted about.

# PARTY GRAZING TABLE

This is a real show-stopper party board – perfect for a New Year's Eve bash or whenever you want to wow some friends! I've included my favourite things to eat and kept it simple so you can buy in everything you need. To give the board some definition it's good to have one or two large pieces to visually anchor the board and then fill the spaces by grouping ingredients together; saving the fruit to add pops of colour at the end. Feel free to add anything else you enjoy! (Pictured on pages 170–171.)

500-g/1 lb. 2-oz. Camembert wheel

200 g/7 oz. Brie

250 g/9 oz. Stilton

250 g/9 oz. Cheddar

400 g/2⅔ cups red grapes, cut into small bunches

400 g/2⅔ cups green grapes, cut into small bunches

100 g/⅓ cup each chutney, relish and pickle of your choice

100 g/3½ oz. sliced serrano ham

100 g/3½ oz. sliced peppercorn salami

100 g/3½ oz. sliced prosciutto

300 g/10½ oz. sliced honey-roast deli ham

3 tbsp mustard of your choice

200-g/7-oz. cured chorizo ring, sliced into chunks

150 g/5 oz. Ardennes coarse pâté

a few good handfuls of rocket/arugula

200 g/7 oz. smoked mackerel

lemon wedges

200 g/7 oz. hummus (see recipe on page 156 or use premade)

300 g/10½ oz. a variety of cheese crackers

285-g/10-oz. jar pickled cornichons and onions, drained

100 g/3½ oz. on-the-vine piccolo tomatoes

100 g/1 cup mixed olives

1 pomegranate, halved

1 grapefruit, halved

2 passion fruit, halved

3 figs

1 baguette, thinly sliced

12 breadsticks

6 mini pork pies

balsamic glaze, to drizzle

## PRESENTATION
*a painted wooden board provides a nice backdrop for all the colours here, but marble also works very well*

**SERVES 8-12**

## HOW TO ASSEMBLE

Start with the cheeses. Place these around the board with the grapes draped around them. Spoon out some of the chutney/relish/pickle into small bowls and place near each cheese (pickle near the Cheddar and relish near the Stilton for example).

Place the charcuterie in groups around the board, fanning out the sliced ham and adding a small bowl of mustard.

Add the sliced chorizo ring and the pâté.

Add a small handful of rocket/arugula and place the smoked mackerel on top along with some lemon wedges.

Spoon the hummus into a bowl and place on the board.

Fan out the crackers in a couple of places and then start to fill any gaps in the board with the remaining ingredients. Keep them grouped together (all the pork pies in one place for instance) and use the fruit to create pockets of colour and boundaries between ingredients.

Dress the remaining rocket/arugula with a splash of balsamic glaze and place in bunches around the board to add freshness.

CHAPTER

# 6

# Sweet Treats

# MINI PAVLOVA TRAY

These individual pavlovas are beautiful to look at and even better to eat; the big time-saver is using pre-made meringues and frozen berries for a super-quick and easy recipe. Feel free to try different berries (frozen cherries are delicious with chocolate shavings) or drizzles of passion fruit pulp and seeds. If you don't want to use freshly whipped cream, you can use a can of fresh squirty cream.

300 g/10½ oz. frozen mixed red berries or other fruit

4 tbsp granulated white sugar

2 tbsp Kirsch or Cognac

600 ml/2½ cups double/heavy cream

1 tsp vanilla extract

4 tbsp icing/confectioner's sugar

200 g/7 oz. strawberries

a few sprigs of mint

10–12 meringue nests

**PRESENTATION**
*a round metal tray with sides is ideal to display the mini pavlovas in a circle*

*disposable piping/pastry bag*

**SERVES 6**

Set aside a few frozen berries to decorate, then mix the rest of the frozen berries with the granulated white sugar and Kirsch or Cognac, and leave to defrost for about 2 hours – the thawing process will create a syrup. Gently mix it all together just before serving.

In a mixing bowl, combine the double/heavy cream, vanilla extract and icing/confectioner's sugar and whisk with a hand-held electric whisk until thick and silky (don't over-whisk or it will go lumpy). Spoon into a disposable piping/pastry bag and store in the fridge for up to 12 hours until ready to use.

Thinly slice one or two of the fresh strawberries vertically and pick a dozen small leaves from the sprigs of mint. Set aside.

When you are ready to serve, place the meringues on a clean work surface and spoon a pile of the thawed berries into the centre of each one. Now pipe the whipped cream around the top of the meringue piping in a circular motion until you have fully encased the berries in the cream. Stick a slither of fresh strawberry and some of the reserved frozen berries in the top of each mound and drizzle some syrup over the top.

**HOW TO ASSEMBLE**
Decant the remaining thawed berries and syrup into a small clean bowl and place in the centre of the tray/board. Arrange the pavlovas around the edge of the tray/board. Fill the rest of the space with the strawberries and add the mint sprigs to decorate. Serve with any leftover cream, if you like.

# DONUT BREAK BOARD

My donut board couldn't be easier. If I'm making this just for the kids I like to use lots of brightly coloured donuts with a few espresso cups filled with hot chocolate and topped with squirty cream. For an adult version, I use donuts of similar shades and swap the hot chocolate for strong coffee (and I'd be lying if I said I never made it an Irish coffee!). Here I've created a board for kids and adults alike. You can simply buy and assemble the board or, if you're feeling adventurous, you can make my mocha dip, which works spectacularly well for that slightly bitter coffee note against the deliciously sweet donuts. (Pictured on pages 178–179.)

250 ml/1 cup hot chocolate (for kids) or strong coffee (for adults)

200 g/1 cup cinnamon sugar (185 g/scant 1 cup caster/superfine sugar mixed with 1 tbsp ground cinnamon)

16 mixed donuts (jam-filled, chocolate-coated, plain rings, etc)

20–30 mixed mini donuts

150 g/1 cup fresh raspberries

150 g/1 cup cherries, stems on

100 g/scant 1 cup salted mixed nuts

4 cinnamon sticks (optional)

**MOCHA DIP**

60 ml/¼ cup full-fat/whole milk

90 g/3 oz. dark/bittersweet chocolate (70 per cent cocoa), broken

2 tbsp freshly made espresso coffee, cooled

**PRESENTATION**
*a large wooden board works well here*

**SERVES 8–12**

**MOCHA DIP**

Heat the milk in a small saucepan and, once it starts to bubble, drop in the broken chocolate and whisk together until the chocolate melts. Finish by adding a shot of espresso coffee and pour into a warm bowl. (Alternatively add the milk and chocolate to a bowl and microwave for 30 seconds, but keep a close eye on it as microwaves do vary. Check after 20 seconds to ensure it isn't burning.)

**HOW TO ASSEMBLE**

Fill some espresso cups with hot chocolate (kids) or coffee (adults) and place on the board. Add the bowl of warm mocha dip to the board. Put the cinnamon sugar in a small bowl and add to the board.

Arrange the large donuts on the board, followed by the mini donuts. Finally fill the spaces with small clusters of raspberries, cherries and nuts. Add a few cinnamon sticks, if liked, just to garnish and for their lovely aroma.

# BUILD-YOUR-OWN
# ICE-CREAM CONE BOARD

A build-your-own cone board is a fab way to serve an easy-going dessert for everyone to enjoy. The fun is all in the making of the flavour and topping combo and letting your creative juices flow. You can put any flavours together to suit your taste; although mandatory for me is the finishing touch of squirty cream and a maraschino cherry on top!

3 x 460-ml/16-fl oz. tubs of your favourite ice cream

500 g/1 lb. 2 oz. ice cubes

6–8 waffle cones

6–8 waffle cups

125 g/1 cup Maraschino cherries

100 g/3½ oz. mini pretzels

100 g/2½ cups mini marshmallows

85 g/½ cup chocolate chips

100 g/½ cup Smarties

50 g/¼ cup sprinkles

8 Oreo cookies

200 ml/scant 1 cup chocolate sauce

200 ml/scant 1 cup strawberry sauce

200 ml/scant 1 cup caramel sauce

200 g/2 cups strawberries

200 g/generous 1½ cups blueberries

3 Cadbury flakes, halved

2 bananas, halved lengthways and widthways, skin on

250-g/9-oz. can fresh squirty cream

**PRESENTATION**
*a galvanized tub sitting on a wooden board*

*ice cream scoops*

**SERVES 6–8**

## HOW TO ASSEMBLE

Place the tubs of ice cream into the galvanized tub, then fill in the gaps around them with the ice cubes to keep them cold and prevent them from melting too quickly. Place this in the centre of the board.

Pile up the waffle cones and cups on the board, either side of the metal tray.

Decant the maraschino cherries, pretzels, mini marshmallows, chocolate chips, Smarties, sprinkles and Oreo cookies into small dishes and place onto the board around the perimeter of the metal tray. Pour the sauces into small jugs/pitchers and add to the board.

Add the remaining ingredients, such as the fresh fruit, placing it directly onto the board and filling up any available space.

Provide ice cream scoops and plenty of paper napkins for cleaning up melting dribbles!

# CUPCAKE BOARD

I'll be honest, I like cupcakes, but for me it's all about that frosting!
You can buy everything pre-made for this board for total convenience,
but if you want to get your hands dirty, I've included a recipe for the
cupcakes, thanks go to my daughter Eva, who is a serial cupcake maker!
And the frosting is stolen from my mum who makes THE BEST-EVER
cream cheese frosting. Now I think about it, I've had very little to do with
this board except the tasting, again and again... I've included a range of
toppings for you to decorate your cupcakes with, but like all the boards,
feel free to add whatever toppings you enjoy! (Pictured on pages 184–185.)

50 g/¼ cup sprinkles

30 g/¼ cup hazelnuts,
roughly chopped

45 g/½ cup sugar flowers

45 g/¼ cup each various
colours and sizes of
sugar balls

50 g/2 oz. white
chocolate

50 g/2 oz. dark/
bittersweet chocolate

60 g/½ cup blueberries
and/or strawberries

## CUPCAKES

120 g/½ cup margarine
or baking spread, at
room temperature

120 g/½ cup plus 2 tbsp
caster/granulated
sugar

120 g/scant 1 cup
self-raising/self-rising
flour

2 eggs (about 120 g/4 oz.)

1 tsp vanilla extract

20 g/scant ¼ cup
unsweetened cocoa
powder

### CREAM CHEESE FROSTING

120 g/1 stick butter, at
room temperature

180 g/generous ¾ cup
full-fat cream cheese

260 g/scant 2 cups icing/
confectioner's sugar,
or to taste

1 tsp freshly squeezed
lemon juice, or to taste

1 tbsp milk (optional)

### CHOCOLATE FROSTING

250 g/2¼ sticks butter, at
room temperature

500 g/3½ cups icing/
confectioner's sugar

50 g/½ cup unsweetened
cocoa powder

a pinch of ground
cinnamon

1 tsp vanilla extract

100 ml/scant ½ cup
whole/full-fat milk

### PRESENTATION

*a light-coloured board to
showcase the colours*

*12-hole cupcake pan,
lined with cases*

*2 piping/pastry bags*

*a vegetable peeler*

**SERVES 6–8**

## CUPCAKES

Preheat the oven to 160°C fan/180°C/350°F/
Gas 4.

Cream the margarine and sugar together with
a hand whisk until incorporated and pale in
colour, then add the flour and eggs into the
mixture, a little at a time, until incorporated.

Divide the cupcake mixture equally between
two bowls. Add the vanilla extract to one bowl
and stir to combine. Fill six cupcake cases with
the vanilla mixture. Add the cocoa powder to
the remaining mixture and fold in. Fill the
remaining six cases with the chocolate mixture.

Bake in the preheated oven for 18–20 minutes,
until they spring back when lightly touched.
Transfer to a wire rack to cool.

## CREAM CHEESE FROSTING

Use a food processor or hand-held electric
whisk to whip the butter and cream cheese
for a few minutes until fluffy. Add the icing/
confectioner's sugar and lemon juice, and
continue whisking until fluffy. If you want it
slightly looser, you can add a splash of milk,
but normally this isn't required. Spoon
into a piping/pastry bag and store at room
temperature until ready to use (if making more
than a couple of hours beforehand, store in
the fridge).

## CHOCOLATE FROSTING

Use a food processor or hand-held electric whisk to whip the butter for a few minutes until fluffy, then add the icing/confectioner's sugar and whisk until fully incorporated. Now add the cocoa powder, cinnamon and vanilla extract, and whisk together. It may look lumpy at this stage, which is when you start to whisk in the milk; do this in stages until the desired consistency is reached. Spoon into a piping/pastry bag and store at room temperature until ready to use (if making more than a couple of hours beforehand, store in the fridge).

## HOW TO ASSEMBLE

Decant the sprinkles, hazelnuts, sugar flowers and sugar balls into small ramekins/bowls and arrange on the board.

Group the cupcakes together on the board, then place the piping/pastry bags around the board.

Create delicate shavings of the white and dark/bittersweet chocolate and add to different spots on the board.

Fill the spaces on the board with pockets of blueberries and strawberries, and sprinkle a few of the sugar flowers and sugar balls in the gaps, if you like.

# BANOFFEE BOARD

I wasn't sure what to call this board; I created it one Sunday afternoon when we all wanted something sweet to eat after dinner and had a pile of bananas staring back at us. It's not sophisticated or glamorous, but it is downright indulgent and lots of fun to eat together. It's evolved over the years, but this is exactly how we serve it at home; occasionally adding some chopped nuts or crumbling Oreo cookies over the top, but I'll leave that to you.

300 ml/1¼ cups double/heavy cream, plus 80 ml/⅓ cup (or use a can of fresh squirty cream, if preferred)

1 tbsp icing/confectioner's sugar

1 tsp vanilla bean paste

50 g/3½ tbsp butter

2–3 bananas, depending on size, peeled and halved lengthways

2½ tbsp brown sugar

125 ml/½ cup peanut butter

125 ml/½ cup hazelnut chocolate spread

a generous pinch of toasted flaked/sliced almonds

3 fresh strawberries, hulled and thinly sliced

a generous pinch of sea salt flakes

**PRESENTATION**
*a marble or ceramic slab works well here as it will keep the cream cool for longer*

**SERVES 4-6**

Whisk the 300 ml/1¼ cups cream with the icing/confectioner's sugar and vanilla bean paste until it forms soft peaks, then store in the fridge until ready to use. Add half the butter to a frying pan or skillet and fry the bananas, cut-side down, for a few minutes until golden, then turn over and fry on the other side for another minute. Transfer to a plate and allow to cool.

In the same pan, add the remaining butter, the brown sugar and the 80 ml/⅓ cup double/heavy cream and bring to a simmer. Cook for a few minutes, stirring frequently, until the sugar is fully dissolved. If the caramel is too thick to drizzle, loosen it with a teaspoon of hot water, then pour into a bowl. Set aside.

**HOW TO ASSEMBLE**
Spoon the peanut butter directly onto the board in big sweeping motions, then do the same with the hazelnut chocolate spread and finally do the same with the whipped cream, spreading it in big swirls.

Place the cooled banana slices on top of the cream, spacing them out evenly, scatter over the flaked/sliced almonds, add the strawberry slices and finish with a drizzle of the caramel over the top and a pinch of sea salt. Serve the remaining caramel on the side.

# INDEX

# ACKNOWLEDGEMENTS

Writing a book is more than the sum of its parts, from the concept and the recipes to the design, styling, shoot, production and editorial that ties everything together, and we haven't got to the poor family members that live with a constant flow of food delivered with the line, "does this taste better than yesterday?"... for five days in a row.

To my wife Anna, who is my harshest critic and the one I trust most, and my children, who take after their mum (and I don't believe a word they say!), I love you all. You're the reason I get out of bed every morning.

I'm lucky enough to spend my authoring career surrounded and supported by incredibly talented people. Every book I've written is a collaboration of ideas, thoughts and hard work, and it's that special alliance of like-minded souls that creates something special and leaves me with a debt of gratitude.

First is David Peters who agreed to let me loose in writing our fifth book together at Ryland Peters & Small – thank you. Julia Charles, Editorial Director, who remains my confidant, therapist, occasional drinking partner and editor, without whom my writing no sense make would it (see what I mean – I did that last line by myself). Thank you Julia, I couldn't do it without you!

Yvonne Doolan, the publicity mastermind who has helped get this incredible book into the hands of so many and always goes above and beyond. The entire design, styling and shoot team headed up by the talented Leslie Harrington, Creative Director, including food stylist Kathy Kordalis, for managing to translate my recipes into beautiful pieces of edible art and putting up with my ramblings on the phone about nothing to do with what she called for, and Lauren Miller for sourcing such beautiful props. And photographer Mowie Kay, for constantly delivering incredible shots and still humouring me that my portraits are not edited to hell and back to make me look somewhat presentable. And finally Patricia Harrington in production, who turns our labours into a printed book you can hold in your hands.

In summary, there are a lot of people who cultivate the germ of an idea sowed around a room into something that blossoms into a beautiful product that we are all proud of, and I couldn't be prouder to know you all.

Theo x